W9-AZV-883

THORNTON WILDER:
The Bright and the Dark

TWENTIETH-CENTURY   AMERICAN   WRITERS

ERNEST HEMINGWAY and the Pursuit of Heroism
by Leo Gurko

RING LARDNER and the Portrait of Folly
by Maxwell Geismar

THORNTON WILDER: the Bright and the Dark
by M. C. Kuner

TWENTIETH-CENTURY AMERICAN WRITERS

THORNTON WILDER:
The Bright and the Dark

By M. C. KUNER

Thomas Y. Crowell Company　　　　　*New York*

813
Kuh

L.C. Card 76-158696
ISBN 0-690-82002-X

1   2   3   4   5   6   7   8   9   10

To "K"

". . . wenn ein treu verliebtes Herz in die Fremde
ziehet . . . ."

CONTENTS

*I want to say to someone . . . that I have known the worst
that the world can do to me, and that nevertheless I praise
the world and all living. All that is, is well. Remember
some day, remember me as one who loved all things and
accepted from the gods all things, the bright and the dark.*

—THE WOMAN OF ANDROS

*Then, welcome each rebuff
That turns earth's smoothness rough,
Each sting that bids nor sit nor stand but go!
Be our joys three-parts pain!
Strive, and hold cheap the strain;
Learn, nor account the pang; dare, never
                grudge the throe!*

*For thence—a paradox
Which comforts while it mocks—
Shall life succeed in that it seems to fail?
What I aspired to be,
And was not, comforts me:
A brute I might have been, but would not sink
                i' the scale.*

—RABBI BEN EZRA, *by Robert Browning*

1 THE SELVAGE:
Biography

Garson Kanin, the American playwright and stage director, once noted a comment made half-jokingly by Thornton Wilder: "I can take care of my immortal soul, but who's going to take care of my laundry?" (When Kanin reported this quip to Somerset Maugham, whose view of the world was diametrically opposed to that of Wilder, Maugham retorted, "If Thornton takes good enough care of his laundry, his soul will take care of itself.") In a sense, Wilder's confidence in the existence of the spiritual verities and in humanity's custodial duties toward them sums him up both as man and artist: his faith is a kind of huge celestial umbrella that preserves him from the harshness of the elements and frees him to focus on such earthly details of everyday life as interest him. Regardless of what he writes, he generally celebrates the music of the spheres and, simultaneously, what he regards as its inevitable counterpoint—the rattle of the dishes.

Thornton Niven Wilder was born in Madison, Wisconsin, on April 17, 1897. His father, Amos P. Wilder, son of a clergyman and a devout member of the Congregational Church, was a Yale graduate who had become a newspaperman and who eventually entered the diplomatic service during the administration of Theodore Roosevelt. His mother, Isabella Thornton Niven, the daughter of the Reverend Doctor James Niven, was a woman equally dedicated to religion and to intellectual pursuits. His elder brother by two years, Amos Niven Wilder, became a professor of theology and the author of several books dealing with the influence of religion on contemporary poetry; a sister, Janet, became a zoologist; another sister, Isabel, became an author (she has written three novels and has also coauthored several articles in collaboration with her brother Thornton), and in later years has generally served as the buffer between him and the world whenever he is engaged in one of his literary projects. Significantly, he dedicated his sixth novel, *The Eighth Day,* to her, for when he retired to the Arizona desert for twenty months, determined to communicate with no one until he finished his work, it was she who looked after his interests in his absence. In her he has found a spiritual twin to compensate for the loss of his actual twin who died at birth.

In 1906 Amos P. Wilder took his family to Hong Kong, where he served as American consul general until 1909. For a short period young Thornton at tended school there—a strict, German-language school—so that at the age of nine he had already been exposed to both the world of the Orient and the culture of Europe, equally alien to all he had previously known. (One wonders how much this early experience contributed to his later artistic interest in exotic settings.) After six months his father sent the family back to the United States, not to Wisconsin, but to Berkeley, California, where Thornton attended the public school. By 1911, when Amos Wilder was serving in Shanghai, the family had returned to China, where Thornton was enrolled first in another German-language school, then at the English Mission School in Chefoo, until 1913. At that time the family came back permanently to California, where Thornton attended the Thacher School in Ojai, graduating from the high school in Berkeley in 1915. At the age of eighteen he had seen more of the world than many people do at forty-eight and he had learned early that a home is based not on a physical location but on human relationships. Not surprisingly, his books have no strong sense of property or of material things; everything he writes is permeated by a vivid feeling for family ties.

When the time came to enroll in college, Thornton chose his father's university, Yale, but Amos Wilder, finding his alma mater too worldly for his son, insisted on Oberlin, a small Ohio college known for its splendid music department and its religious character. At Oberlin young Wilder began writing seriously; in his two years there he contributed several pieces to the literary magazine. In addition, he was fortunate enough to study with Charles Wager, a teacher with a passion for literature who kindled the imagination of his students. Wager's interests, which, unlike those of some academic minds, were not narrowly confined to a minute area of specialization, struck a responsive chord in Wilder, for Wager's learning ranged over many countries and epochs. It was probably from him that Wilder developed his own intuitive appreciation for the writings of the past, for tradition, for history, for legend. And Wilder's natural inclination in this direction was supported by precedent: both Shakespeare, who represented the end of an era, and George Bernard Shaw, who represented the beginning of one, deliberately selected for their material subjects and characters that had already been explored by artists before them. Perhaps what most impressed Wilder was the discovery that genuine masterpieces are timeless: in the words of Wager, "Every great work was written this morning," or, in modern parlance, is relevant.

At Oberlin, too, Wilder first came into contact with that school of criticism known as the new humanism. A number of American critics, among them Irving Babbitt of Harvard, had grown contemptuous of the parochial kind of naturalism characteristic of American literature. Such writers, for example, as Theodore Dreiser, who appeared to scrutinize only the petty, sordid, materialistic details of everyday life, seemed to the humanists to be abandoning all that was best and most intelligent in man, to be concentrating on the gutters instead of the stars. They felt that tradition in the form of Christian orthodoxy and in the great classics provided the answer to literature and to life; books that stressed despair and deprivation could contribute nothing of lasting value. This was a view that the young Wilder found very easy to accept, for his religious inheritance on both sides of the family, in addition to his very strict upbringing, his freedom from financial burdens, his lack of contact with physical discomfort or pain, his distance from emotional crises—all insulated him from the harshness of the world and caused him to give emphasis to the life of the mind and the spirit. It was at Oberlin that his character and temperament first took definite shape.

In 1917 Wilder transferred to Yale, a move that was not entirely to his father's satisfaction; about the same time, the latter resigned from the consular service and with his family took up permanent residence in New Haven. At Yale Wilder interrupted his education for eight months in order to serve with the First Coast Artillery at Fort Adams, Rhode Island; though he did not see overseas duty during World War I, he at least participated in his country's involvement with it, as he was again to do later, in World War II. Leaving the service as a corporal, he returned to Yale in 1919 and, the following year, earned his Bachelor of Arts degree.

In 1920 Wilder went to Europe on a fellowship and studied at the American Academy in Rome. It was there, he tells us, that one of the most memorable experiences of his life came to him: as a member of an archaeological team he helped excavate an Etruscan street, buried centuries ago. And suddenly his awareness that this lost civilization, which had existed even before the Romans, had collided with his own moment in time clarified and confirmed all his previous thought processes: there was no past, present, or future to be considered separately; no geographical limitations could be taken seriously when an ancient culture could be laid bare by a modern American shovel. As he was later to explain it in *The Eighth Day:* "It is only in appearance that time is a river. It is a vast landscape, and it is the eye of the beholder that moves."

His year in Rome not only gave Wilder material for his later works, such as *The Woman of Andros* and *The Ides of March,* both rooted in antiquity, but also provided him with the philosophical basis for all his writing. But once again his father intervened and summoned him home, for the elder Wilder had secured a position for his son as a teacher of French at the Lawrenceville School, an excellent preparatory school near Princeton. He taught there for four years, eventually becoming master of Davis House at the school, and spent his free time writing and, in the summers, traveling. He took a leave of absence between 1924 and 1926 in order to earn a Master of Arts degree in French at Princeton, during which time he was still writing and studying on his own, as well as contributing to, and helping to edit, the magazine *S₄N.* He spent the summer of 1925 at the MacDowell Colony in Peterborough, New Hampshire, a center founded by the widow of the composer Edward Alexander MacDowell to encourage writers, artists, and composers to work in a setting congenial to them. The near-wilderness of the colony, the isolation of its members from each other except during the evening communal meal, served to free them from the noise and pressure of the outside world and enabled them to concentrate on their projects without interruption. In future years Wilder was to seek out this sanctuary repeatedly in order to complete his novels and plays.

As we shall see, one of Thornton Wilder's outstanding qualities has been his talent for compartmentalizing his interests. Thus his easy, pleasant surroundings while he was studying at Princeton did not entice him, as they have so many others, from his creative writing efforts, nor did the drudgery of correcting French "themes" at Lawrenceville dry up his inspiration. On the other hand, his determination to become a writer never interfered with his teaching: he was, by all accounts, a good and a popular one. (It must be remembered that unlike writers who enter the academic world after earning their credentials in the field of fiction or journalism and who deliver popular lectures on literature as "lions" of the campus, Wilder was a workaday teacher who was not liberated from the more pedestrian demands of his profession by a glamorous reputation; he had yet to win it.) When we consider further that he took his graduate degree one year before producing his first novel, we can appreciate the fact that Wilder-the-Scholar enriched rather than intruded upon Wilder-the-Author. To this day, his life, more than that of any other artist, exemplifies this triune principle of Creator, Teacher, Student.

The year 1926 proved to be a turning-point: in the spring he published his first novel, *The Cabala,* and in the fall he saw a production of his first full-length play, *The Trumpet Shall Sound* (written during 1919–20, when he was still at Yale), by the American Repertory Theatre in New York. The following year (1927) *The Bridge of San Luis Rey* appeared, and it was far more warmly received than the previous novel: as a matter of record, in its first year there were thirteen printings in Great Britain, while over 100,000 copies were sold in America. This popular success was capped by an artistic triumph—the two seldom go together—for in 1928 Wilder was awarded the Pulitzer Prize for fiction. And in the same year his collection of three-minute sketches called *The Angel That Troubled the Waters and Other Plays,* some of them written when he was still in high school, also appeared. It was quite clear that as a professional author he had "arrived." Determined to devote his energies to writing, he resigned from Lawrenceville. But the move was more a shift in emphasis than a change in roles: whereas he had been a teacher who wrote in his spare time, he now became a writer who taught in his spare time.

As many children do, Wilder had written little sketches in which he, his sisters, and his friends could act; unlike most, however, he did not outgrow this interest in drama but continued to work at it through high school and college. Whenever he could he attended the theater in Oakland, although the best he could see there was usually a farce or a romance of small distinction. (In fact, some of these plays, totally old-fashioned in structure and using butlers and serving maids to explain the action to the audience, impressed him enough to have him lampoon their defects in two of his own comedies, *The Matchmaker* and *The Skin of Our Teeth,* years later.)

But if he was unable to find worthwhile theater on the stage, there was always the library to instruct him. He read plays omnivorously until the opportunity arose to study the "living theater" seriously. By 1928 his financial position, which had always been a safe one, was so secure, thanks to the growing sales of *The Bridge of San Luis Rey,* that he and his sister Isabel left America for a two-year tour of Europe. Together they sent back articles to *Theatre Arts Magazine,* describing what they had seen on the continental stage: in sixty-three days, they noted, they had attended fifty-two productions, surely some kind of a world's record. Wilder was deeply impressed by the brilliant productions of the Austrian director Max Reinhardt at the Theater in der Josefstadt in Vienna. Later he was to adapt the farce *Einen Jux Will Er Sich Machen* by Johann Nestroy, a nineteenth-century Viennese writer, into *The Merchant of Yonkers,* unsuccessfully directed by Reinhardt in America; to put it aside for sixteen years; and to transform it finally into *The Matchmaker,* which, in its musical form, *Hello, Dolly!,* probably earned more money for Wilder than all of his other books and plays added together.

His theater journal proves a revelation of his tastes. He detested Franz Wedekind's *Lulu,* although he admired the production, for the Austrian dramatist's exploration of his sordid heroine's psyche alienated Wilder, who was never at home with tormented characters tasting the dregs of life. On the other hand, two operas, more than all the others, enchanted him even though their productions left something to be desired: he wrote feelingly of Beethoven's *Fidelio* and Mozart's

The Magic Flute. Fidelio, a young woman who dresses as a boy in order to follow her unjustly imprisoned husband and who finds work in the gaol while attempting to free him from a political tyrant, surely represents, especially as realized by Beethoven's magnificent music, that element of the human spirit most cherished by Wilder: fortitude, endurance, the determination of the human race to survive despite all obstacles. And *The Magic Flute,* which celebrates the union of two lovers who pass through incredible trials and tribulations before they are found worthy to enter the "holy portals" of wisdom and forbearance, is a kind of hymn to the mind and heart of man, a theme which Wilder never tires of exploring. That these two operas must have had a genuine impact on him is clear when one considers an episode from *The Eighth Day,* written almost forty years later: a young man who has left home under unhappy circumstances and come to Chicago to make a career for himself as a reporter, who has no real knowledge of, or interest in, music, is given free tickets to many operas. And which does he find most unforgettable? *Fidelio* and *The Magic Flute.*

Wilder's stay abroad was not only a learning process for him; it was a period when he developed lifelong friendships with some of the most distinguished men and women of the day. Like all Americans of that period, he went to Paris; unlike most of them, however, he went not as one self-exiled from his native land, after the style of F. Scott Fitzgerald and others, but as one at home whatever his surroundings. In short, his sojourn was not an escape but an adventure. Among others, in Paris he met Sylvia Beach, the friend and publisher of

James Joyce; in Vienna, Sigmund Freud, who deeply admired *The Bridge of San Luis Rey;* and in London, Lady Sybil Colefax, a brilliant society hostess (the uncharitable called her a lion-hunter), an interior decorator and stage designer (her most notable achievement was the setting for John Gielgud's 1944 revival of Somerset Maugham's comedy *The Circle*), wife of an eminent lawyer and member of Parliament, and, although more than twenty years older than Wilder, his closest friend until her death in 1950.

Since Wilder's interests were always many and varied, he struck up an improbable friendship with Gene Tunney, perhaps the only boxer in history with a passion for literature (to be sure, there is Muhammad Ali), and the two set out on a walking tour of France and Italy. According to Glenway Wescott, the novelist and friend of Wilder, whenever Tunney happened to hear Wilder mention a good book, he bought it; before long he was staggering under the weight of a rucksackful of volumes. When they arrived in England they called on George Bernard Shaw, who in his youth had boxed and had written a novel on boxing. There is something inherently funny in the idea of the great Irish writer wishing to discuss the fine points of the fighting game while the great American champion of the ring thirsted to debate the virtues of the classics; Wilder, however, seems to have taken it all quite seriously. It was left to the humorist Robert Benchley to compose a parody of the scene later, with Tunney talking highbrow English while Shaw lapsed into the jargon of Madison Square Garden.

Upon his return to the United States in 1930, Wilder

called on Scott and Zelda Fitzgerald at their home, Ellerslie, where he also made the acquaintance of the American critic Edmund Wilson. Fitzgerald had praised Wilder highly, preferring *The Cabala* to *The Bridge of San Luis Rey* and informing Wilson that the young author was a man of great and rare talent. Since Wilson felt that these novels were a trifle precious and fragile, he guessed that their author would be the same, but instead of the aesthete he expected, he met a man who proved to have "positive, peppery" opinions. On another occasion at the Fitzgeralds', when a party was being given in honor of Zöe Akins, the American playwright, everyone, Wilson observed, was floating on scintillating conversation and good wine—except for Wilder. He was certainly having as fine a time as everyone else, but he remained, in Wilson's words, "sharply and firmly non-soluble." Wilson has here put his finger on the nature of Thornton Wilder: his manner, friendly on the surface, has behind it a reserve that cannot be broken down; his books and plays, full of humanity and kindness, have nevertheless a detachment that suggests their creator's habit of standing apart from life.

Although Wilder plunged into the stream of social activity in 1930 and, in the same year, built himself a house in Hamden, just outside New Haven, Connecticut, where he still lives, the pleasures of success did not deter him from finishing a new novel, *The Woman of Andros,* which proved to be a great disappointment to his admirers. Based on a play, *Andria,* by the Roman master of comedy, Terence, Wilder's novel, which was set in pre-Christian Greece, seemed to many an evasion of, and an escape from, the crisis America was passing through: the stock-market crash, which threatened to engulf Europe's economy as well. (How much America's withdrawal from financial commitments in Germany helped to demoralize that country still further and make it ripe for the ideology of Adolf Hitler remains an open question with some historians even today.) From one end of the United States to the other, well-to-do and even wealthy families were ruined overnight; men killed themselves every day, some because they could not face the wreck of their fortunes, some because their insurance was the only way of providing security for their wives and children. There were bread-lines and soup-kitchens everywhere, and everywhere there was fear for the future. In such an atmosphere it was difficult to understand what had prompted a man of Wilder's taste and sensitivity to fashion a graceful tale of long ago. But despite the sometimes scurrilous attacks on him, he kept his silence and went his own way.

Wilder accepted an appointment at the University of Chicago as a lecturer in comparative literature, free to hold classes during one semester of an academic year so that he could devote himself to writing during the other semester. The post interested Wilder enough for him to remain until 1936; during that time he completed a collection of plays, *The Long Christmas Dinner* (1931); a novel, *Heaven's My Destination* (1935); and a translation of *Lucrèce* by the French playwright André Obey, adapted for the American actress Katharine Cornell and produced on Broadway in 1932. He also found opportunities for two cross-country lecture tours, spent one semester at the University of Hawaii as a visiting professor, and dabbled in screenwriting, for which he received no film credits. This six-year period seems to have been a preparation for the burst of activity that was to follow.

The critical attacks on *The Woman of Andros* must have made Wilder realize that he was out of touch with his native land. Perhaps it is not accidental that *The Long Christmas Dinner* was his first published work to characterize the "American Way," while *Heaven's My Destination,* also native in setting, humorously revealed that most American of types, "the do-gooder." It is not too much to say that the idealistic, troublemaking hero of Graham Greene's *The Quiet American* is the logical descendant of Thornton Wilder's George Brush, the hero of *Heaven's My Destination.* If Wilder's life had so totally protected him from understanding the anguish of the American catastrophe emotionally, at least he could apprehend it intellectually; it is to his eternal credit that he learned to profit from the public rebukes he suffered and turned them to his artistic advantage.

In addition, the change of scene to Chicago was a sharp contrast to the kind of teaching he had been engaged in at Lawrenceville. First of all, he was dealing with older, more mature students and was not responsible, as in a preparatory school, for disciplining them. Secondly, he was no longer in an academic town such as Princeton or New Haven, with a graceful campus and a cloistered atmosphere, but in a sprawling, teeming city crammed with different ethnic groups and social classes, a city whose university drew students from every walk of life. And finally, instead of being part of an institution steeped in all the traditions represented by the "old school tie," Wilder was now attached to one that was being revitalized and reshaped by a fellow Yale alumnus two years younger than himself—Robert Hutchins, whose theories, based on the belief that qualified high school students should be admitted to a university at the end of their second year, were revolutionizing higher education. As in earlier years, Wilder proved to have excellent rapport with his students, occasionally joining them for an evening of conviviality.

The intellectual environment in Chicago must have been considerably more heady than that of the other places in which Wilder had been accustomed to teach and learn. In the 1930's the city had already earned its right to be considered the second cultural capital of the United States, for such writers as Carl Sandburg, Theodore Dreiser, Sherwood Anderson, and Sinclair Lewis had celebrated (or damned) it in verse and fiction and given it a literary immortality; Wilder himself was to make the Chicago of an earlier era a focal point of *The Eighth Day.* But in addition to the new world that Chicago opened to Wilder, it was also responsible for an important meeting between him and another writer, Gertrude Stein, who was to have a marked influence on his work, as indeed he proved to have on hers.

Gertrude Stein was by then an almost legendary figure. A woman of independent means who had left her native America and settled in Europe in 1903, she gathered together some of the most famous authors and artists on two continents, launched a number of careers, and established herself as the center of the intellectual life of Paris. Any young American writer coming to Europe for the first time called at her flat on the rue de Fleurus—where she lived with her secretary and alter-ego, Alice B. Toklas—almost as a matter of course, almost as a debutante, wishing to be presented at court, might be expected to seek a sponsor. Some young writers, like Ernest Hemingway, gladly accepted her friendship, then outgrew it and quarreled with her; some rejected her from the beginning as the leader of the intelligentsia (Somerset Maugham was known to have called her "an old Roquefort cheese"); and a very few, a minority, like Wilder, maintained their esteem for her throughout her life, although she was a difficult person to endure.

Oddly enough, Wilder had never met her during his trips to Europe; unlike Hemingway, Fitzgerald, and Wescott, he had not deliberately uprooted himself from his native land in order to write about it, and so, not looking upon himself as an expatriate, perhaps he felt small inclination to join the circle and meet its patron saint. Whatever the reason, Wilder and Miss Stein did not encounter each other until she returned to America in 1934, her first visit in thirty-one years, in order to give a series of lectures at the major universities and colleges. At Wilder's invitation she stopped at the University of Chicago to deliver her speech on "Poetry and Grammar" and proved so popular and stimulating a speaker—one is tempted to parody a comment of Oscar Wilde's about himself and say that Miss Stein put her genius into her talking and her talent into her writing—that President Hutchins invited her to return to Chicago at the end of her tour, which she did. On both occasions Wilder obligingly lent his apartment to Miss Stein and Miss Toklas, and his consideration, unfailing courtesy, patience, and obvious interest in Miss Stein's writings established an enduring friendship.

His constant championing of her books (he wrote introductions to three of them) was quite genuinely based on an admiration for them; one suspects, however, that the admiration was, in part, based on his gratitude for what he had learned from her. In a letter to her in 1935, he expressed his thanks for the freshness of her viewpoint: "I am a slow-poke plodder in so many ways, still stuck in the literal 19th century—but very proud every time I feel I have made more progress." This is not the false, self-deprecating modesty of a writer fishing for a compliment, but the honest statement of a craftsman aware of his shortcomings and trying painfully to correct them. Possibly the strongest idea Miss Stein had impressed on Wilder was her notion of time and mobility and the ways both could be put to work in American literature. Since Wilder was himself already interested in these problems, it wanted only a small push in the right direction, provided by Miss Stein, to launch him on the themes and techniques that were to occupy him in the years ahead.

It is possible that the two years Wilder spent abroad touring and studying European theaters were responsible for turning his attention to the stage in the late 1930's; it is also true that his earliest written pieces were in the form of short plays, indicating his inclinations in that direction. Wilder has himself stated that he considers the theater the greatest of all art forms, "the most immediate way in which a human being can share with another the sense of what it is to be a human being." And so, after his first contact with Broadway through his translation of *Lucrèce,* he abandoned the domain of the novel for a time in order to concentrate on the drama. His circle of friends began more and more to consist of distinguished theater names: Katharine Cornell, who starred in *Lucrèce;* Alexander Woollcott, bon-vivant, drama critic, and member of the Hotel Algonquin's illustrious Round Table, which included such writers as Robert Benchley and Dorothy Parker; Ned Sheldon, the playwright who had fallen victim to paralysis and blindness at the very height of his career, but who encouraged his theater friends to visit him and to read him their plays (Robert Sherwood describes an evening in which Alfred Lunt and Lynn Fontanne acted out Sherwood's *There Shall Be No Night* for Sheldon and profited from his advice); and perhaps most important for Wilder's future at that moment, Jed Harris, one of Broadway's most talented director-producers. Seeking a vehicle for Ruth Gordon, the gifted American actress and author, Harris suggested that Wilder prepare a new version of Henrik Ibsen's *A Doll's House,* which opened on Broadway to lukewarm reviews; Miss Gordon was perhaps not the ideal choice for the heroine, Nora. Still, the meeting with her was to have handsome rewards in later years, for when Wilder rewrote an unsuccessful

comedy of his and called it *The Matchmaker,* it was Miss
Gordon who brought to the role of Dolly Levi the
qualities most needed for a rollicking farce.

After these unsatisfactory jousts with the commercial
theater, no one was prepared for what happened on
February 4, 1938, the New York opening of *Our Town.*
It had been well received at its Princeton premiere on
January 22, but fared badly in Boston; the wife of the
governor of Massachusetts informed the box office that
it was "too sad," and there was, according to Wilder
himself, a good deal of "sobbing and nose-blowing."
When Harris brought it to New York ahead of schedule,
since its Boston reception had proved too depressing
and there was nothing to gain by keeping it in that city,
there was much anxiety about the play's chances for
survival. Glenway Wescott reports that Wilder asked
him if he thought the play was worthwhile; he wanted to
know whether he had disgraced himself, whether the
emotions were too "outspoken and common." While he
rapped out these questions, Wescott noticed that Wilder
was trembling slightly, all the way up from his knees.
Wescott, who admired the play, nevertheless felt that it
would not do well at the box office, for it was too
"delicate, too philosophical, too sad." In fact, it not only
proved a commercial blockbuster on Broadway but was
made into a successful film in 1942, and at that time
producers were much more concerned about remaining
faithful to the property they had bought than they had
been a few years earlier, when the film version of *The
Bridge of San Luis Rey* was badly bungled. Furthermore,

Our Town proved as popular in the theaters abroad as it had been in America, especially in Germany, where Wilder was much admired.

It was at this point in his life that he became interested enough in acting to substitute for Frank Craven, who played the Stage Manager, on Broadway for a fortnight, and to appear the following summer on the "strawhat" circuit. He took great pleasure in a 1943 production of *Our Town* at the Yale Drama School, which used both students and faculty members. At the time the distinguished American drama critic Walter Prichard Eaton played the Stage Manager (Wilder offered advice on the performance, perhaps the only time a writer has been in a position to advise a critic about anything), and Samuel Bemis, the prize-winning historian, played, not surprisingly, the professor who lectures on dinosaurs. There must have been an extra fillip for Wilder, as a Yale alumnus, in watching the production of his own play on his old campus.

The critical carping that had pursued Wilder ever since he wrote *The Woman of Andros* had, in a way, dimmed his reputation. Even after he published *Heaven's My Destination* as an answer to the reproaches for his "escapism," he was still viewed with suspicion as a writer who had failed to be responsive to his country's voice. Even so staunch an admirer as Edmund Wilson was shaken. But *Our Town* was Americana at its best. It was not unlike Eugene O'Neill's *Ah, Wilderness!* in its evocation of turn-of-the-century New England; it was a trifle unconventional in technique, thereby attracting those who might otherwise have been disdainful of the play's "folksy" message. Above all, since it reiterated the enduring values of the human spirit at a time when Europe was perched on the edge of a volcanic eruption and a new barbarism was sweeping the world, *Our Town*, with its faith and affirmation, touched almost everyone. When it was awarded the Pulitzer Prize in 1938, there were only a few dissenting voices, among them the Drama Critics' Circle, who bestowed their prize on John Steinbeck's *Of Mice and Men*, a play they felt to be more realistic and more representative of the age. Curiously enough, *Our Town*, which was considered ahead of its time and experimental in technique, seemed in a recent production—a successful revival in 1969, starring Henry Fonda as the Stage Manager—very much a romantic period piece, just as *Of Mice and Men*, viewed as a television play in the same year, seemed in its rugged brutality a perfect expression of the message-conscious 1930's. Despite the charm of the one and the power of the other, they both have the air of museum pieces, for the passage of thirty-two years has forced us to regard them from a historical perspective.

Wilder, who until the success of *Our Town* had been considered a member of the intelligentsia, suddenly found himself the author of a "smash" and therefore, willingly or not, a member in good standing of "show biz." He was pursued incessantly by reporters, who published the most trifling details of his life as though they were front-page news; before he had found time to catch his breath he was being besieged by journalists demanding when his new play would be finished; he was interviewed, photographed, and quoted interminably. To some extent the experience must have been pleasing, but since Wilder has always been a very private kind of man, in the end he must have found these publicity hounds a nuisance. Yet he proved, both then and afterward, his good humor, patience, and tact by trying to oblige the press while keeping aloof. The world learned no more of his personal life than it had known before, for he gave them the trappings of information only. The essence of Thornton Wilder is more to be found in his writings than in all the pronouncements made by others in all the gossip columns ever printed.

On December 12, 1938, *The Merchant of Yonkers* opened in Boston for the usual trial run before its New York premiere. The play, based on a farce by Johann Nestroy, who in turn had adapted it from a nineteenth-century English farce by John Oxenford called *A Day Well Spent,* had suffered innumerable difficulties almost from its inception. Wilder had written it originally for Ruth Gordon, who was unwilling to act in it unless Jed Harris would direct her; Harris, however, had not been offered the play, partly because he was a nerve-racking person to work with, even for one of Wilder's equable temperament, and partly because Wilder wished Max Reinhardt, whom he had for a long time deeply admired, to direct it. This American version of a Viennese farce seemed the perfect choice for the Austrian director-producer, whose name had long been associated with imagination and originality in the theater and who had helped to revive Austria's lost glory after World

War I by organizing the Festival at Salzburg, where he
and Wilder had met.

Unhappily, while Reinhardt had a good command of
English, he was not at home with the American acting
style, which, particularly in comedy and farce, is quite
different from that of the German theater: stage business and manners which might seem funny to a German
audience might well be considered overdone by Americans. And since comedy depends for much of its effect
on timing and pacing, the difference between the two
cultures might constitute the difference between failure
and success. Another difficulty was in the casting. Jane
Cowl, the Dolly Levi of the play, was an actress known
for her airy comedy technique, most skillful in plays of
drawing-room manners. This role required a kind of
coarseness or, at least, toughness, a kind of strident
charm that was simply not in her repertoire. And
finally, while *The Merchant of Yonkers* did not differ
appreciably on the surface from the revised version
Wilder was to offer in 1954 as *The Matchmaker,* the
latter, probably through the efforts of the new director,
Tyrone Guthrie, bore no trace of the mawkishness and
didacticism which had flawed the earlier work. Though
most critics tend to credit Guthrie and Miss Gordon
with the success of *The Matchmaker,* implying that
heavy-handed directing and unwise casting were alone
responsible for the failure of *The Merchant,* a close study
of both texts indicates that Wilder had improved the
writing the second time round. *The Merchant of Yonkers,*
however, closed after twenty-eight performances.

Wilder took the defeat in good part, generously

dedicating the printed version to Max Reinhardt regardless of where the blame fell, and he began to occupy himself with another play, called *The Emporium,* that he hoped to offer Jed Harris. Wescott tells us that though it was completed, it was never released by Wilder, who was dissatisfied with the results. Whenever something he writes fails, it is not because he has been in a rush to get it into production or publication, come what may; he is a meticulous craftsman and a patient one, who will not pass on to others what does not meet his own high standards. In his own words, "A writer's best friend is his waste-basket and his worst enemy is his couch."

Casting around for another dramatic idea, Wilder began to study James Joyce's novel *Finnegans Wake,* exploring its possibilities as a stage piece. Meanwhile, world events were more and more crowding upon him. In 1941 he made a good-will tour of South America sponsored by the U.S. State Department; then, as an American delegate to the International Society of Poets, Playwrights, Essayists, and Novelists (P.E.N.) he defined the meaning of democracy in a world overturned by devils of cruelty who disregard the rights of the individual. Within a few months Pearl Harbor had been attacked, and now America was at war. He enlisted shortly afterward and became a captain in Army Air Corps Intelligence, pleased to serve his country and, at the same time, convinced that the experience would benefit him as a writer, since he would be thrown among very different types from his literary and theatrical friends. But before he left, he entrusted to his sister

Isabel the manuscript on which he had been working for three years: it proved to be his next play, *The Skin of Our Teeth.* Just before his departure he had completed his only full-length film script for that master of suspense, director Alfred Hitchcock. *Shadow of a Doubt,* Alexander Woollcott tells us, was really finished on a train going from Los Angeles to New York—a 3,000-mile journey during which Hitchcock talked over the final details with Wilder and took notes from him. Film critics generally consider this a minor classic; it certainly proved popular enough to be remade with a different cast some years later.

The Skin of Our Teeth, meanwhile, suffered a few minor setbacks. First, Jed Harris, after reading the script, had no faith in it and turned it down. Then, Helen Hayes, one of America's first ladies of the theater, for whom Wilder had designed one of the three starring roles, also declined. Finally, an unknown young producer named Michael Myerberg was offered it, and, as a longtime admirer of Wilder, he accepted with alacrity. Tallulah Bankhead, as famous for her skill in comedy as in serious drama, took over the role meant for Miss Hayes (and gave one of the most distinguished performances of her career), while stage and screen star Frederic March and his wife, Florence Eldredge, played Mr. and Mrs. Antrobus. The director was Elia Kazan, probably a much more fortunate choice than Jed Harris, for Kazan's forte, from plays like *Camino Real* to *Death of a Salesman,* has always been the less conventionally structured, less orthodox type of drama that frees him to experiment with styles. Although Wilder's comedy baffled some critics and earned the dislike of others, it was successful, and after it opened in New York on November 18, 1942, it settled down for a run. By that time, of course, Wilder had been shipped to North Africa for war service; shortly thereafter he was sent to Italy, where he remained until the war's end in 1945, when he was discharged as a lieutenant-colonel.

Within two months of the play's opening, an article written by Joseph Campbell and Henry Morton Robinson, authors of *A Skeleton Key to Finnegans Wake,* appeared in two installments in the *Saturday Review of Literature.* Calling their piece "The Skin of Whose Teeth?", they attacked Wilder for plagiarizing from Joyce's novel by using the Irish writer's style and ideas. In meaning if not in word, they questioned Wilder's integrity as an artist. The storm raised by this controversy was far greater than the earlier one which had impugned his sensitivity to the American scene when he published *The Woman of Andros;* as before and as always, Wilder remained silent. Battle lines were drawn up: Edmund Wilson, a longtime admirer of Wilder, defended him from the charge; an equally distinguished drama critic, George Jean Nathan, sided with Campbell and Robinson; while another, Harrison Smith, felt Wilder had "pulled a fast one on the public and especially those dramatic critics who received his play with mixed, but in some cases, wild enthusiasm." As a result of the unpleasantness, the Drama Critics' Circle did not award him their prize for that year, although the play was far and away the best of the season; but a few months later *The Skin of Our Teeth* won the Pulitzer Prize, making Wilder a recipient for the third time and so dulling the noise of the dissenters. Since Wilder's literary pattern has been consistently to utilize the myths and materials of times past, it seems unfair to accuse him of theft; as he once told Glenway Wescott, "I am never ashamed of my imitations. I reel from intoxication to intoxication." And Wescott goes on to quote another writer on the subject, Paul Valéry, who said, "Nothing is more original, nothing truer to oneself, than to feed upon others' minds. Only be sure that you digest them. The lion consists of assimilated sheep." Wilder's comedy certainly achieved this goal.

For the next few years, from 1945 to 1948, Wilder devoted himself to lecturing, publishing essays, traveling, supervising productions of *The Skin of Our Teeth* abroad, and even acting the role of the central character, Mr. Antrobus, in September 1946. Of this performance Glenway Wescott has a most vivid memory, for he ranks Wilder's interpretation of the part with Laurence Olivier's Coriolanus and with Laurette Taylor's Amanda in *The Glass Menagerie.* If the praise sounds a little excessive, it is because Wescott felt that the person of Wilder and the character of Antrobus had blended so completely that it was impossible to tell where real life ended and make-believe began. Wilder seemed to be playing himself—or at least everything he had ever believed in concerning the survival of the human race. The portrait was "exalted, yet ordinary," once again demonstrating his concept of the universe as a mixture of the sublime and the average, even the ridiculous. His acting was tied to his writing: "polished and purposeful . . . plain and modest."

These years were not so much a time of literary effort

as an opportunity to garner well-earned awards. In addition to receiving the Bronze Star and the Legion of Merit from the United States, Wilder enjoyed honorary officership in the Order of the British Empire, while his alma mater, Yale, conferred an honorary doctorate upon him in June 1947, in an impressive ceremony also honoring John Hersey, the novelist, and Viscount Alexander, the British general. It was during this period that Wilder became friends with Jean-Paul Sartre, leader of the existentialist movement in France, and it is probable that Sartre's influence on him contributed much to his next novel, *The Ides of March* (1948), a re-creation, in letter form, of the last days of Julius Caesar. Some critics were disappointed that he had "retreated" to the past again; some admired the erudition but felt the book lacked warmth and feeling; some objected to the liberties taken with historical fact; the reviews, in short, were mixed. Yet some, Glenway Wescott among them, thought this the finest work Wilder had ever produced, the one most calculated to earn him immortality, and the only one which bore traces of a skepticism, even a pessimism, seldom associated with Wilder. In 1963 the book was adapted into a drama, but although the leading roles were played by such international stars as John Gielgud and Irene Worth, it failed in its Edinburgh production and was not brought to New York. Its form was too introspective for the theater—surely the reason why Wilder had conceived it as a novel.

In the same year Wilder translated Sartre's *Morts sans Sépulture,* a drama of the French resistance; under the title of *The Victors,* it was presented off-Broadway, where it was only politely received. (Regardless of his translator, Sartre has almost never enjoyed a commercial success in America, except perhaps for his *Huis-clos,* or *No Exit;* he is considered too "talky" for Broadway audiences.) But Wilder had no connection with this production, since he had already left for Germany to deliver some lectures. Later, back in Aspen, Colorado, he delivered a lecture on Goethe on the occasion of the two-hundreth anniversary of his birth; during the academic year 1950–51 he was Charles Eliot Norton Professor of Poetry at Harvard, probably the most distinguished visiting professorship that exists in America; this time he confined his lectures to exclusively native talents like Melville, Thoreau, and Emily Dickinson. In the same year he gave a paper on the seventeenth-century Spanish dramatist Lope da Vega before the Modern Language Association of America, an organization of teachers of language and literature. A group more removed from a Broadway author of "hits" would be impossible to imagine, yet Wilder was perfectly at home with his former colleagues, for he had never really left the profession. He was made a member of the Légion d'Honneur; he was the recipient of the Gold Medal for Fiction given by the American Academy of Arts and Letters; Northwestern and Harvard Universities bestowed honorary doctorates on him; UNESCO (the United Nations Educational, Scientific, and Cultural Organization) designated him to head the American delegation at a meeting in Italy; the State Department, in a rare move, sent as the official American entry to the International Theatre Festival in Paris a production of *The Skin of Our Teeth,* this time starring Helen Hayes. In this period it became difficult to tell when

Wilder was traveling for pleasure and when he was stopping somewhere to collect an award.

In the summer of 1954, possibly gently prodded by Garson Kanin and Ruth Gordon, he revised *The Merchant of Yonkers* and retitled it *The Matchmaker*. On this occasion Tyrone Guthrie, as skillful at directing knockabout farce as Shakespearean tragedy, held the reins, while Ruth Gordon proved everything Wilder dreamed she would be in the role of Dolly. Eileen Herlie, who was to enchant audiences in Guthrie's production of *The Makropoulos Secret*, took the role of Mrs. Molloy; Alec McCowen, later to be seen in *Hadrian VII*, played Barnaby and was later followed by Robert Morse, who in a few years would achieve renown in *How to Succeed in Business without Really Trying*; and Arthur Hill, the future George of *Who's Afraid of Virginia Woolf?*, as Cornelius rounded out an exceptional cast. Presented first at the Edinburgh Festival on August 23, 1954, and transferred to London before it opened in New York in December 1955, *The Matchmaker* proved an irresistible success, dismaying some intellectuals who felt that Wilder had stooped to conquer, but delighting the general public. Shirley Booth later starred in the film version of the play, also directed by Guthrie.

When it became the musical *Hello, Dolly!* Carol Channing was the first of a long line to sing the lead, and almost every eminent performer in the different media has appeared in it: stage stars like Mary Martin and Ethel Merman, and, in a spectacular production, Pearl Bailey with an all-black cast including Cab Calloway; screen stars like Ginger Rogers and Betty Grable; and television stars like Phyllis Diller. When Hollywood bought the rights to the musical, Barbra Streisand played the title role. At present, *Hello, Dolly!,* which is also enjoying a huge success abroad, bids fair to outrun almost every other musical in history. The most attractive aspect of Thornton Wilder's career is that he has managed to charm both the highbrows and the lowbrows, though not always at the same time. Very few writers can make such a claim.

In the summer of 1955 Wilder, who had relished his collaboration with Guthrie (and there is scarcely a playwright who has felt anything less than worship for Guthrie's patient understanding of a new script), completed an adaptation of Euripides' *Alcestis,* called, for the Edinburgh production, *A Life in the Sun,* although Wilder had preferred the title of *The Alcestiad.* The play starred Irene Worth, and it was unsuccessful, although the German-speaking public professed to admire it when it had its German-language debut in Zurich and later was done in Munich; it is probable that esteem for the author rather than enthusiasm for the play prompted its friendly reception. It was set to music by the American composer Louise Talma and produced in 1962 at Frankfurt-am-Main, where it was greeted respectfully. Composers seem to be more interested in Wilder's work than in that of other American authors, for Paul Hindemith has set to music *The Long Christmas Dinner* (Wilder himself provided the libretto), and Herman Reutter has fashioned an opera from *The Bridge of San Luis Rey.*

For the next ten years Wilder busied himself with writing essays and short plays. Two of them were produced in Germany as a double bill: "The Wreck of the

5:25" and "Berniece," but they were poorly received and remain unpublished. His three new one-act plays appeared off-Broadway at the Circle-in-the-Square Theatre during 1962; they were part of what was to be a double cycle of dramas. One cycle consisting of seven plays was to represent the seven deadly sins; the other, the seven ages of man. Of the first group, Wilder completed "Someone from Assisi," a dramatization of the sin of lust; of the second group, Wilder offered "Childhood" and "Infancy." Collectively entitled *Plays for Bleecker Street,* a reference to the area in Greenwich Village where the theater was located, the bill was presented by José Quintero and Theodore Mann, who had done so much to revive interest in Eugene O'Neill's dramas and to produce successfully in their playhouse such Broadway "failures" as *The Iceman Cometh,* Tennessee Williams' *Summer and Smoke,* and Truman Capote's *The Grass Harp.* Probably Wilder entrusted his plays to Quintero and Mann because of his deep respect for their dedication to the best in theater and their determination to place art above commerce.

After the opening in March 1962, Wilder determined to withdraw to the Arizona desert for two years and devote himself to the completion of both cycles of plays. The announcement brought forth a constant stream of interviewers armed with such questions as "Where, why, when, and how." An article in *The New York Times* carried the heading, "Wilder to Relax in Desert 2 Years," and since it is the spirit of the age to assume that anyone seeking solitude and contemplation is something of a curiosity, an eccentric, his decision gave rise to a large amount of publicity, precisely what he was trying to avoid. Consequently, after fulfilling a White House invitation to read some of his works, he simply disappeared without giving anyone specifics about his whereabouts, except for his sister Isabel, the only one who knew how to reach him if the necessity should arise. He remained in his desert retreat for a year and a half, not even coming to Washington to receive the Presidential Medal of Freedom that had been awarded him. Shortly thereafter he decided to lay aside the project he had been working on and to concentrate on a novel that, it would seem, was a byproduct of his original idea for the two cycles of plays. And so he left the desert and, the following month, sailed for Italy to continue with the book. As usual, reporters pursued him; the *Times* noted, "Hideaway in Italy Chosen by Wilder." He refused all further communication with the press even upon his return to America at the end of 1964, and disappearing again, finally finished the project. It was published in 1967, its title *The Eighth Day.* It received only moderately enthusiastic reviews, although the critics appeared to appreciate the monumental task Wilder had set himself—it was the longest work he has ever written.

In accordance with his customary pattern, he has spent the years since publication of *The Eighth Day* in traveling, visiting old friends, and, no doubt, contemplating another literary project. What Thornton Wilder once wrote of Thomas Mann applies equally well to himself: "He was methodical in work and of great industry."

2 THE FABRIC:
Early Efforts

When *Our Town* first appeared in 1938, Sir Cedric Hardwicke, the well-known actor, said that he loved the play because Thornton Wilder had asked of the theater "nothing more than four walls and lights." As early as his undergraduate days at Oberlin, and even before, Wilder had demonstrated his preference for a theater that left almost everything to the imagination, that encouraged the spectator to conjure up his own vision of what a particular setting should look like, that permitted the actor to pantomime business instead of working with actual objects or props. The theaters of China and Japan had always used such devices; for example, an Oriental actor making his entrance carrying a whip would be understood by the audience to be on horseback. The best of children's theater follows much the same principle, since young audiences have fertile imaginations that they lose all too often as they grow older. At any rate, both the sophistication of Eastern and the simplicity of youthful audiences have this in common: they are a much more collaborative element in the theater than the usual passive spectator separated from the performer by a picture-frame stage that attempts to copy reality.

It must be understood that any current artistic movement is in one way a reaction to what has gone before. Thus the early nineteenth century poets and painters who glorified nature and the emotions, who were labeled "romantic" in their approach, were simply protesting against what they thought to be the extreme artificiality and restraint of an earlier day; in their own minds they must have considered themselves highly realistic reporters of the truth as they saw it. As time passed and their style began to appear too sentimental to the next generation, they were superseded by those who, in their turn, became the apostles of another, entirely opposite kind of realism.

The new movement of the later nineteenth century was inaugurated by Gustave Flaubert in the novel and by Henrik Ibsen on the stage. Flaubert's *Madame Bovary,* for example, became a classic of factual reporting: it recorded the world of a middle-class woman who yearns for a Prince Charming to bring color and excitement to her life and who cannot appreciate the solid, if drab, virtues, of her adoring husband. She rejects him to pursue a futile dream, which, in the end, destroys her. Flaubert here portrayed the romantic illusions and the moral weakness of those who refuse to face reality.

In much the same vein, dramatist Henrik Ibsen examined popular concepts of the day and showed their bankruptcy. *A Doll's House* presents a supposedly ideal marriage between a seemingly strong husband and a weak, doll-like wife, but in the end proves the courage of the woman who renounces her marriage and her husband's values in order to discover her own identity. (The female protagonist, Nora, is certainly an early heroine of the Women's Liberation Movement.) In *Ghosts* Ibsen studies the way in which society forces people into conventional modes of behavior, warps their true nature, and even wrecks their lives.

A German playwright of the day, Gerhart Hauptmann, described the economic suffering of laborers displaced by the Industrial Revolution in his drama *The Weavers.* The Swedish dramatist August Strindberg devoted the early part of his theatrical career to an examination of the relationship between the sexes in such plays as *Miss Julie* and *The Father;* and again and again he demonstrated the struggle for power that forever divides men and women, regardless of the sincerity of their passion (years later, the American playwright Edward Albee would make this theme the heart of his celebrated drama *Who's Afraid of Virginia Woolf?*). In France Eugène Brieux was exposing the corruption of the legal and judicial system in his drama *The Red Robe,* while in Russia Anton Chekhov was to write tragicomedies of a decaying upper-middle class that would yield eventually to a more vigorous lower class on the way up. His compatriot Maxim Gorki, in his drama *The Lower Depths,* would soon show the world how grinding poverty and society's indifference brutalized the castoffs of the universe—yet all the same they were just as capable of feeling anguish as any hero of Greek or Shakespearean tragedy, and just as worthy of the audience's understanding and compassion.

The literature of this period, then, dealt largely with problems besetting the middle and lower classes and with psychological or economic difficulties. The technique was that of a camera impersonally snapping photographs (garbage cans on street corners were as legitimate a subject for the pictures as flowers in the park); the concentration was on the petty details that reflected everyday life. Before long this interpretation of life so dominated Europe and the United States that, as late as the 1940's and 1950's, one American play called for a refrigerator that made real ice *(The Voice of the Turtle)* and another for a real swimming pool into which the actors could plunge *(Wish You Were Here).* This obsession for reproducing "real life," which, incidentally, the innovators like Ibsen had long since abandoned, maintained a strong hold on the American theater; it would be safe to say that a number of commercially successful plays on Broadway even today are still cast in a mold that seems outworn and confining for the age.

For some reason Thornton Wilder never came under the spell of this type of realism: when the angry young men of the 1920's were hurling their thunderbolts against political and social injustices in imitation of Gerhart Hauptmann and Henri Becque, Wilder was attempting plays that were religious in theme and unrealistic in form.

The Trumpet Shall Sound, his first play, which he wrote

as a Yale undergraduate, concerns a man named Peter
Magnus who leaves his Washington Square mansion
(the time is the end of the nineteenth century) for a
business trip, charging his servants to care for the place
while he is away. During his absence his butler dies, and
one of the maids, Flora, in conspiracy with the remaining servants, rents out the premises to thieves, cut-
throats and associated undesirables, hoping that one of
the vacant rooms will be taken by a young sailor, Carlos,
with whom she is in love. Although he does not return
her passion—and the theme of unrequited love is to
crop up often in the works of Wilder, from *The Cabala*
to *The Ides of March*—he goes through a form of
marriage service with her. Before long Peter Magnus
returns unexpectedly, and when he sees what has
happened to his house he asks the police for permission
to try all the tenants individually, in order to assess the
degree of their guilt. This sounding of the trumpet, this
day of judgment, is agreed to by the police; after
Magnus questions each of the characters he decides that
despite their wicked lives they are all worthy of forgiveness. The other servants fix the blame for the entire
proceedings on Flora, and she, abandoned by the man
she loves, kills herself with his pistol.

Wilder's idea might suggest that God in His infinite
mercy, in the person of Magnus, can forgive even those
who have committed serious sins; possibly only Flora,
who has been guilty of the unpardonable sin of despair
in taking her life, is beyond redemption. The text might
also be seen as an ironic commentary on those who
presume to judge, like Peter Magnus—the implicit

message being that only God has the right and the wisdom to do so. Either way the intention is blurred. Furthermore, the symbolism is too obvious (the rooms are always cold, yet the heaters are always smoking, like an apartment in Hell); the ending with Flora's suicide is too illogical. There is little in the play, except for occasionally effective dialogue, to indicate the author's coming stage triumphs. What makes it valuable, however, is that it introduces the reader to Wilder's ideas about the content of a play and about his approach to drama. Significantly, his latest, uncompleted cycle of plays, *The Seven Deadly Sins,* like *The Trumpet Shall Sound,* rests on a theological base; despite the passage of almost half a century between the two works, his signature tune is still the religious parable.

Because of its symbolic, antirealistic approach, *The Trumpet Shall Sound* caught the attention of the director Richard Boleslavsky, who produced it in New York seven years after it was written, in 1926. Boleslavsky, who had been trained at the Moscow Art Theatre in the days of its greatest influence, was deeply interested in scripts that drew upon the inventive powers of the actor. One of the exercises he devised for his students was the telling of a story, a depicting of the day's activities entirely without props. This technique is, of course, no longer novel, but half a century ago, when the emphasis was more on realism and when the theories of Stanislavsky, the Russian actor and producer, were still considered experimental in some quarters, Boleslavsky's teaching was innovative.

Actually, the question of how to build a character has

constantly divided actors into two camps. Those who
rely only on the externals of a magnetic personality and
physical and vocal grace generally impose themselves on
the role without surrendering their identity. The
French tragedienne Sarah Bernhardt was of this school,
in the opinion of George Bernard Shaw when he served
as a drama critic. Those who submerge themselves in
the part so much that it is impossible to distinguish the
character in the drama from the person who is performing are less external in their approach; rather, they
look inward for something in their own natures that
would help them to project the truth about the character. The great Italian actress Eleanora Duse followed
this path. One might contrast the two by saying that the
public would see Bernhardt *in* some play but would see
Duse *as* some character.

Both methods, of course, have their virtues. The
hopelessness of deciding which is superior is perhaps
well typified by a story of two distinguished British
performers appearing in a play called *Edward, My Son* in
the 1950's. Robert Morley received high praise for the
"realistic" manner in which he almost strangled his stage
wife, Peggy Ashcroft, while she, in turn, enjoyed great
adulation for the way she reacted to being choked to
death. When an interviewer asked Miss Ashcroft how
she had achieved her effect she said that as an admirer
of Stanislavsky she had sought for, and finally remembered, an incident in her childhood of near-drowning;
she tried to recapture that sensation of going under for
the third time when she was on the stage. When the
interviewer put the same question to Mr. Morley, he

noted that he hadn't been thinking of anything in particular at that moment of violence; as a matter of fact, he was feeling very pleased about the boxoffice receipts!

Nevertheless, Stanislavsky's teachings and writings, which formalized his ideas and spread them throughout the theater world, demanded of his actors simplicity and imagination and psychological truth at a time when these elements were sorely needed. His philosophy, carried out by Richard Boleslavsky, struck a responsive chord in Thornton Wilder. Much later, when he came to write *Our Town,* his script called for the housewives to shell imaginary peas and for the young lovers to sip imaginary sodas through imaginary straws, leaning on a counter formed by placing a wooden slat over two high stools. As he was to say, "The drama is based upon pretense."

If *The Trumpet Shall Sound* was not theatrically effective—and one of its weaknesses was its excessive length—his next collection, *The Angel That Troubled the Waters,* was composed of pieces that were much too short. Several of them were written in college; all were deliberately conceived as three-minute plays. Although published later, in 1928, most of them were marred by a youthful preciousness of language and an insubstantiality of structure. Yet again, they contained the same themes that continue to preoccupy Wilder today, and all of them were concerned with a moral conflict. In his preface, after pointing out that almost all the plays were religious in tone, Wilder indicated that they might serve a useful instructive purpose in an age of literature when religious writing was not too well understood or too welcome. For his part, he felt that to write this kind of drama well would be to write the best kind of drama that existed.

The most arresting quality in this collection of plays is the scope of the subject matter. Characters like the Virgin Mary and St. Joseph, Christ, Satan, Judas, Mozart, Gabriel, Shelley, Ibsen, and a talking donkey named Hepzibah people the various plays; the periods range from Biblical times to Renaissance Paris to eighteenth-century Vienna to nineteenth-century Wales (typically, twentieth-century America is not represented); the settings move from Heaven to the prow of a ship to a goldsmith's shop to a peasant's cottage; and the themes concern themselves with the relationship of the artist to the universe, the meaning of morality, the nature of salvation, the necessity for recognizing beauty in the world, and the importance of living life to the full. When one considers the type of play that Wilder was writing at almost the same moment Eugene O'Neill was producing dramas like *Before Breakfast,* in which a shrewish wife drives her husband to offstage suicide while she is preparing their meal in a shabby, run-down kitchen, one begins to appreciate the individuality of Wilder's vision; before long a large number of aspiring American playwrights would model their dramas first after those of O'Neill, then after those of Clifford Odets, and, in succeeding years, after those of Arthur Miller, Tennessee Williams, and Edward Albee, all of whom owed a heavy debt to realism. Only Wilder remained apart from this vogue.

The first play in the collection is called "Nascuntur Poetae." A Boy is looking at the paintings of Piero di Cosimo when a Woman wearing a chlamys (a short, oblong Greek mantle fastened with a clasp on the shoulder) enters and tells him he was chosen for a great enterprise. She gives him her presents of Pride and Joy. Soon after her sister, a Woman dressed in deep red, appears and gives him a gold chain, a leaf of laurel, a staff for his journey, and a crystal. The Boy symbolizes the soul of the poet; the chain binds him to his responsibilities as an artist; the laurel proclaims his affinity with Apollo, God of Poetry; the staff aids him on his pilgrimage, for he is, by the nature of his calling, predestined to have no permanent home; and the crystal ball gives him the power to see visions beyond the capacity of ordinary men. The Boy is unwilling to accept these gifts, but he has no choice: it is thus, as the title indicates, that poets are born.

The nature of the artist is studied in "Centaurs"; here the character of Shelley addresses an audience that has just seen Ibsen's *The Master Builder*. Shelley explains that he has wanted to write a poem about the death of a centaur. At this point the character of Ibsen interrupts to say that he took Shelley's idea and shaped it into *The Master Builder*, which is also about the death of a centaur, half-man, half-horse, or, in Ibsen's rendition, half-man, half-visionary. Wilder's theme, of course, is that the same materials are used again and again; that writers are drawn to similar subjects, although they clothe their ideas in different raiment; that, in fact, nothing is new under the sun—except, perhaps, the unique way in which the artist regards his world. And since the centaur is a creature woven into a myth by the Greeks, Shelley, an early nineteenth century British poet, can rework the story, and Ibsen, a late nineteenth century Norwegian dramatist, can reinterpret it. In this way, the past and the present mingle: the classics inspire the romantics; the romantics inspire the realists; countries separated by frontiers become one under the canopy of ideas; and time, place, and civilizations are like vast rivers emptying into the seas, which, in turn, flow into the ocean. Despite the theatrical impracticability of "Centaurs," Wilder makes it one of the mosaics of a later, far more effective play, *The Skin of Our Teeth.*

The function of the artist is explained in "Mozart and the Gray Steward." According to legend, when Mozart lay ill, he received a visitor who commissioned him to write a requiem; as time passed Mozart grew more and more convinced that the man in gray was Death and that he was composing his own requiem. Wilder uses this story as his starting point: Mozart is instructed not to sign his name to the piece, which is to be composed in memory of a dead countess, but to make it look as though the requiem were the work of the grieving widower, Count von Walsegg. Naturally Mozart refuses to allow anyone else to take credit for what he has done, and so, in a dream, the Gray Steward tells him that the work has indeed been commissioned by Death himself. Mozart is to give voice to all those millions sleeping who have no one but him to speak for them. "There lie the captains and the thieves, the queens and the drudges . . . only through the intercession of great love, and of great art which is love, can that despairing cry be eased." But why has Death chosen the countess, who was a silly woman in her lifetime, to be the vessel of this musical grandeur? Because "all her folly has passed into the dignity and grandeur of her state." There is an echo here of the transformation of Emily in *Our Town* after she has come back to visit the living, of the change from the ordinary to the supremely wise. Finally, Death tells Mozart that although he is a great composer he should kiss the slippers of the foolish noblewoman, for "only he who has kissed the leper can enter the kingdom of art." Christian humility blends with artistic accomplishment in order to create something great.

Another group of playlets links religion and philosophy. "Childe Roland to the Dark Tower Came" deals with a figure out of literature and is set on a Flemish moor. Roland, who is wounded, seeks shelter and aid, but he is rejected. At the end, when he is dying, he acknowledges the beauty of death; only then is he given admission to the castle. From a religious and orthodox point of view, his resignation can be described as "making a good death," as accepting God's will. From a philosophical or aesthetic point of view, he is accepting death as another figure in the pattern, as something that completes the whole and is therefore artistically necessary. This is the real beauty of death, and only when it is viewed in such a manner can it give life any meaning, can humanity be admitted to the castle. This theme is also recurrent in Wilder's more seasoned plays and novels.

In "Leviathan" a young Prince who has been cast upon the Venetian shore after a shipwreck encounters a mermaid. He thinks he is dreaming when she asks him for his soul and promises him whatever he wishes in return. He refuses her request, for to surrender his soul is to renounce his individuality. Then a sea-monster, Leviathan, devours him. But even though he has died, the mermaid feels that a part of the Prince's soul, his uniqueness, hovers in the atmosphere. In the Christian sense, he has returned to the Spirit which is God; he has been absorbed but not obliterated. As a character is to say in *Our Town,* "Something is eternal, and that something has to do with human beings."

One of the pieces is a marionette show entitled "Proserpine and the Devils." According to classical legend, Proserpine, daughter of Demeter, the Goddess of the Harvest, was snatched away by Pluto, God of the Underworld, who then made her his queen. In Wilder's version all these characters are puppets worked by magicians, while Proserpine, instead of being a modest, gentle, obedient girl, is strong-willed and aggressive. It is she who hurls herself at Pluto, instead of the other way around. Suddenly the manipulators begin to argue violently, and as the quarrel grows more and more heated the scene breaks down and the puppets collapse. An Archangel falls to the pavement; Pluto (or Satan) rolls into the lake. The mixture of pagan and Christian characters in this play is another of Wilder's favorite gambits: in *The Woman of Andros* the Greek heroine has a prevision of the birth of Christ; in *The Cabala* one of the young men of modern Rome is a reincarnation of

Pan. Finally, the manner in which the puppets affirm their reality only to be exposed as wooden dolls indicates Wilder's awareness of truth as interchangeable with illusion; he employs this device with comic effectiveness in *The Skin of Our Teeth.*

Four of the plays contain Biblical characters and raise questions about faith versus reason, hope versus despair, joy versus suffering, self-importance versus humility. "Now the Servant's Name Was Malchus" takes place in Heaven where "the nebula are born . . . and the stars, the clockwork of the sky." Christ is watching one star in particular, the earth, which is in need of redemption; as it turns on its axis, it sighs (a difficult stage-direction!). Malchus recalls that when he was alive he was the servant of the High Priest and had his ear cut off by St. Peter. What bothers him most is that whenever the Biblical story is read during Holy Week, he is made to look ridiculous. He asks Christ to have his name removed from the book. Christ tells him that he, too, feels ridiculous, for he thought that after his death he could be useful to men, but they believed him to be either crazy or deceitful. "My promises were so vast that I am either divine or ridiculous." Malchus is still unhappy about his situation and remarks that the Bible wasn't even right about *which* of his ears had been cut off. And Christ observes, "The book isn't always true about me, either. . . . Malchus, will you stay and be ridiculous with me?" Malchus must choose between his "image," his preoccupation with self, and the world of Christ, the spirit of selflessness. He chooses the latter, for he has gained, in death, a wisdom that he did not have before.

"Hast Thou Considered My Servant Job?" is a reinterpretation of the betrayal of Christ. After Christ's return to Heaven, Satan expresses joy because the earth rejected him; Satan's great favorite is Judas, the instrument of the Prince of Darkness. In thirty hours Satan expects to seal all men to him, and he boasts that none will betray him, as they did Christ, for "I build not on intermittent dreams and timid aspirations but on the unshakable passions of greed and lust and self-love." Suddenly Judas hurls the thirty pieces of silver through space, and coming before Satan curses him, arraying himself finally on the side of Christ. The devil cannot understand what has happened to change Judas' thinking, since he can never grasp the truth that the mercy of Christ can prevail over the Kingdom of Hell. But love, believes Wilder, has the power to transform even the traitor Judas into a true follower of Christ.

In "The Flight into Egypt" the chief role is taken by a talking donkey name Hepzibah. She is carrying the Virgin Mary and the Child Jesus into Egypt, and as she trots along she discusses the problems of faith and reason. She wonders why some die, like the infants massacred by Herod, and why some live; and as she ruminates on the scheme of things she moves more and more slowly along the road. When Mary reminds Hepzibah that she is carrying the Lord, she argues that she will do everything she can "within reason," but again she slows down, because she is afraid of meeting crocodiles in the swamp. Debate seems more important to her than intuitive faith. She tells Mary that she is the leader of a girls' group that has "very interesting religious discussions" and would like to have some information to carry back to her friends. Mary's only answer is, "Do just as I do and bear your master on," indicating that nothing is as important as serving the will of God. Again and again Hepzibah takes up various issues: ironically, although she knows she is living at a great moment in history, she cannot cure herself of hairsplitting. Too often man, like the donkey, faced with the grandeur of God's design, can only utter banalities. And as Hepzibah speaks, behind her the scenery unrolls on a revolving cyclorama: the Tigris, the Euphrates, the pyramids, the Sphinx pass by. This blending of the stream of time with the details of everyday life is, even at this early point in his career, a hallmark of Wilder's style.

The last play in the collection gives its title to the whole volume. "The Angel That Troubled the Waters" takes place near a pool around which the ill and the dying congregate in order to be cured. Many of them are, among them a Mistaken Invalid; but one Newcomer is denied a healing. He is a physician who wants to be restored not in body but in spirit. Since he looks healthy enough, the invalids tell him that he does not belong there, but he insists that he is suffering from a guilt from which he must be cleansed if he is to continue his work. The angel refuses him his wish; it is the fate of the one who heals to remain sick himself. "It is your very remorse that makes your low voice tremble into the hearts of men. The very angels themselves cannot persuade the wretched and blundering children on earth as can one human being broken on the wheels of living. In Love's service only the wounded soldiers can serve." This theme of suffering and its necessity in the army of God becomes a major idea in both *The Bridge of San Luis Rey* and *The Woman of Andros*. Closely tied to such a concept is the Christian belief in self-abnegation, which becomes the "Open, Sesame" to the portals of Heaven. There is an old legend that perfectly illustrates Wilder's point. If one looks at a view through clear glass one can see everything outside. But once the glass is silvered by egotism, it turns into a mirror that allows one to catch only one's own image.

In one way or another, these plays contain the seeds of almost all Wilder's future subjects. They reveal his impatience with the confining aspects of realism and his need to move freely in space and time. They mix myth with parable, classical tradition with religious orthodoxy. They stress his interest in abstracts rather than concretes, in philosophical rather than purely human considerations. And therefore they lack characterization, suggesting the technique of the early artists of the Middle Ages, flat and one-dimensional. (Even at the height of his skill, Wilder never produced more than two memorable characters in his novels and perhaps two in his plays—and only then because of very special circumstances.) But they show the stamp of an original, or, at the very least, an individual talent.

The major weaknesses are those of form and diction. The plays read more like fairy tales than theater pieces, the dialogue could hardly be spoken by actors. But these were minor hurdles for Wilder the Student. His solution was hard work and self-discipline, "the passionate assimilation of a few masterpieces written from a spirit somewhat like his own, and of a few masterpieces written from a spirit not at all like his own." To this end, Wilder read everything that Cardinal Newman, the nineteenth-century British theologian, had written and then everything that Jonathan Swift, the eighteenth-century British essayist, had written, gaining support for his own ideas from the first and learning how to toughen and simplify his style from the second. He believed that it was possible to acquire a technical understanding of literature "almost unconsciously on the tide of a great enthusiasm, even syntax; even sentence-structure; I should like to hope, even spelling." When the years of his apprenticeship were over, he had pretty well realized his goals.

3 THE WARP THREADS: Time Past

Glenway Wescott has observed that Thornton Wilder likes things to seem traditional, to "hark back to the entirety of beloved accumulated literature" as a way of proving that every modern idea has its origin in the thoughts of great writers, just as every current activity is rooted in the deeds of those who lived long ago. Since his training and education owed much to classical civilization, it is not surprising that the first three novels he wrote were either set in remote periods of time or in a foreign land.

Like his best comic novel, *Heaven's My Destination,* and his most recent one, *The Eighth Day,* Wilder's first novel, *The Cabala,* begins on a train (trains, bridges, ships, all the symbols of arrival and departure, of physical impermanence, are characteristic of Wilder's settings) steaming toward Rome late at night. A young American, fresh from the university, crammed full of theoretical knowledge but totally ignorant of life, muses on the year he is to spend in this magic city, a perfect fusion of the pagan and the Christian. He has traveled very little and therefore can only imagine what Rome (and the world) is like. Needless to say, by the end of the book he has had a rude awakening, for he has encountered reality.

While on the train, the narrator, known only by the name Samuele given him later by his Roman friends, first hears of the mysterious group called the Cabala. The name itself is strange: does it have any reference to a certain body of Hebrew religious lore? Is it some sort of secret political society? At first Samuele is unable to learn anything: he has no more illumination than has the starless night above him. Gradually, as he becomes acquainted with the Cabalists—and they accept him only because they discover that he is of a "good" family, even if he is American—they confide that they are a group dedicated to the past and to the conservation of tradition. That they prove to be shallow and their goals worthless makes them only the more grotesque and pathetic; they are, in fact, dinosaurs in the world in which they live. For the book itself is set in the year 1920, immediately after a world war that in many ways, if not in the loss of life, was more devastating than World War II. Three mighty empires—the Austrian, the German, the Russian—had collapsed, and with their collapse all semblance of order, however tyrannical, had vanished; the erosion of British and French influence and power throughout the world had begun; and in the wake of these disasters a great wave of despair had swept over Europe. At a time when imagination and fresh ideas are desperately needed, all the Cabalists can conceive of is burying their heads in the sand and dreaming of the good old days, for all the world like children thrusting their fingers into the holes of a dike that is hopelessly cracked.

The other American in the book, Samuele's friend James Blair, characterizes the Cabalists as people "getting what comfort they can out of each other's excellence." The irony is that despite the limitations of their vision and their inability to accept the times in which they live, they *are* superior people: they have excellent minds, high standards, a deep appreciation of literature and art, a rare capacity for love and devotion. Yet they never learn how to make use of their talents; their lives end in frustration and tragedy, and the reader is left thinking, like Othello, "O the pity of it!"

Wilder's use of Samuele reveals what is to become his favorite device: a narrator who moves in and out of the lives of a group of characters, who serves as a catalyst, and who generally holds the book together. Since Wilder seems to prefer the episodic structure in his novels (and plays), the narrator (or stage manager) can also perform another function: as commentator rather than active participant, he stands between the main characters and the reader (or audience), thus creating an effect of distance and detachment. As a result, Wilder's style has about it a cool serenity that from the beginning set him apart from his literary contemporaries.

Samuele, both in the prologue and the epilogue, seems to suggest still another value: the "innocent" American in confrontation with the "wicked" (or sophisticated) European, a formula that Henry James, whom Wilder much admired, had often employed with great skill and perception. But James, being a pre–World War I author, was bound to be on the whole highly partial to the Europeans, while Wilder, as a post–World War I author, was more skeptical. Despite its past grandeur, Europe in 1920 looked very much like the morning after the night before; it was now America in Wilder's estimation that seemed to hold promise for the future.

The three sections of the book are concerned with the three major figures whom Samuele meets: in each case he tries to help them; in each case he fails, not so much because of his inadequacies as because of their predestined ruin. (In a way, the novel suggests the predicament of the characters in Anton Chekhov's *The Cherry Orchard:* the Ranevskys—the privileged class—are constantly being told by Lopahin—whose father was a serf on their land—what they must do to save themselves and their property. So the Cabalists are offered advice by the New World in the person of Samuele; like the Ranevskys, they cannot take it, for they, too, are incapable of confronting the fact that their world is doomed.)

To set the tone of the novel, on Samuele's first evening in Rome his friend Blair takes him to visit a young poet who is dying. As the location is described— an apartment near the Spanish Steps—and the Englishman's malady—consumption—the reader is instantly aware that the poet is John Keats, who actually had died exactly a century before. Already past and present are jumbled. Thereafter Samuele comes into the lives of certain members of the Cabala and, directly or indirectly, changes them.

The leader of the Cabala, Miss Grier, arranges for Samuele's invitation to Tivoli (in a house where the villa of the ancient Roman poet Horace once stood) and to the Villa Colonna (the Colonnas were a prominent family during the Renaissance); again Wilder unites classical with Christian Rome. At the end of the book Miss Grier voices the suspicion that Samuele has become Mercury, the messenger of the gods, whose other function is to lead the dead to Hades, an indication of the tragedies that befall the three characters Samuele meets. But Wilder's choice of the name Samuele is significant from another point of view: it recalls the prophet and judge of the Old Testament, who was also the link between the dying monarchies of the past and the ideal kingdom of the future, represented by David.

Samuele's first encounter is with the sixteen-year-old son of the Duchess d'Aquilanera. Representing the past in her conservative ideas and in her ancestral pride, the Duchess wishes to assure herself that her son, Marcantonio, will continue the family tradition; to that end she has arranged a suitably aristocratic marriage for him. But Marcantonio, a kind of Pan, has led such a corrupt and dissolute life, despite his youth, that he has become the scandal of Rome; worse still, he is imperiling his marriage by his behavior. Driven to despair, the Duchess implores Samuele to help influence her son to a better life: she is convinced that Samuele's blameless behavior and Puritan philosophy will impress Marcantonio. In a way, they do: "It is the libertine and not the preacher who conceives most truly of purity." And so Marcantonio seems to renounce his pursuit of women (whom he really despises anyway as beings without souls) and instead turns to the athletic life, determining to train for the Olympics. But ingrained habits die hard and he grows tired of the sacrifice. In the end, torn and confused, he seduces his half-sister, Donna Julia, and, in horror, kills himself. Ironically, his body is discovered by a pushy American, Frederick Perkins, who has been so anxious to meet important European aristocrats that he has all but broken into the villa to attain his goal; and it is Perkins' intrusion that robs poor Marcantonio's death of the dignity it might have had. To cap all, the incredibly stupid Duchess, a loving mother but an imperceptive human being, is convinced that her son perished because of his "conversion" to purity. She never learns the truth.

There is high comedy in Samuele's advice to the lustful Marcantonio to exercise as a means of cooling his passions: the American has no concept of what is driving the Roman. Samuele, of course, is full of good intentions, like George Brush of *Heaven's My Destination;* and like George he understands little about the flesh. As he sees it, to run around the block and take a cold shower is to restore sex to its proper perspective; part of the delight that Marcantonio takes in the chase, the capture—and the corruption—is beyond Samuele's experience. So this encounter, which first began in the darkness of night, ends in failure: the Marcantonios of this world, like the decaying characters in Thomas Mann's *The Magic Mountain,* will not survive to carry on the name.

Samuele's second encounter is with Alix, the lovely Princess d'Espoli, who falls desperately in love with his friend, the American archaeologist James Blair. Alix, whose husband is surely what Marcantonio would have become had he lived, has an unhappy capacity for falling in love with men who do not return her passion: in Marcel Proust's wry aphorism, "The love that lasts longest is the love that is never returned." Driven to despair, she contemplates suicide: it is her tragedy that with her intelligence, her sensitivity, her humanity, her talent for bringing out the best in people, she should be obsessed by a frozen stick of a man, a pedant who "knew everything about Michelangelo yet never felt deeply a single work . . . who studied the saints and never thought about religion. His endless pursuit of facts was not so much the will to do something as it was the will to escape something else." Finally, she tries to put her life in order and resumes her social activities, but this time in a hectic manner that indicates she has not been cured. She seeks relief by consulting a magician, a seer (these sessions also take place in the night); on this occasion she meets Blair accidentally, he bows to her politely and leaves. She assumes the pretence of indifference and returns to her friends in the Cabala. Samuele, as baffled by her passion as he was by Marcantonio's sensuality, believes that she has rid herself of her madness, but much later, when she hears Blair's name spoken, she faints. And Samuele's efforts to turn her from her hopeless longing fail.

In the third episode Samuele is working on a play about St. Augustine when he goes to the villa of Marie-Astrée-Luce de Morfontaine. Astrée-Luce, unlike the others, is deeply religious; her dream is to see the monarchy (tradition) restored in France under Catholic rule, for she senses that Europe is dying and feels that nothing but faith can save it. She involves Samuele in her efforts to persuade a powerful churchman, Cardinal Vaini, once a missionary in China, now a political figure at the Vatican, to help. The Cardinal recognizes that she is good but not very intelligent, intuitive rather than rational, and without consciously meaning to hurt her, systematically embarks on a subtle campaign to wreck her faith. Just as Marcantonio and his family represented the decaying aristocracy, the Cardinal represents a dying Church in the sense that it cannot or will not respond to contemporary needs. The Cardinal is so successful in his plan that he drives Astrée-Luce to despair and she tries to shoot him, denouncing him as the devil who has robbed her of her faith. Only then does he understand what a hairsplitter and sophist he has become, how far he has drifted from true religion. Repentant, he renounces his worldly life and sets out for China, hoping to recapture the idealism he had known when he was young. But he dies at sea—far from his goal.

The last section switches suddenly from reality to fantasy. Samuele, now on board a ship bound for home, has an imaginary conversation with Virgil, not only the greatest of the Roman poets but the one most admired by Christians in the Middle Ages. Virgil, who admires Milton more than Dante, but who most admires Shakespeare because the latter was in life "neither the enemy nor the advocate of grace," tells Samuele that once he believed Rome was eternal. But Virgil knows better now: "Nothing is eternal save Heaven. Rome is dying. Seek out some city that is young. The secret is to make a city, not to rest in it. When you have found one, drink in the illusion that she too is eternal." And Samuele's boat sails on to America, the future, this time under a sky covered with bright stars.

The novel is a combination of themes to which Wilder is to return again and again. There is love for the past and for tradition; there is also the balancing idea that intellect and tradition, grown cold, bring no contributions to the world and can even cause disaster. There is the flow of time in the choice of Rome as the backdrop for the tragedies—in this sense truly the Eternal City. And there is the American on his physical and spiritual journey, adding the vitality of the future to the loveliness of the past.

If the book deals largely with the decline of the West as played out by the three sets of characters, it also raises other questions. Marcantonio, representing the flesh, tries to become spirit. He fails. Alix, representing the mind, tries to lose herself in the flesh. She fails. Astrée-Luce, representing the religious spirit, tries to become reason. And she fails. All three, in encountering their opposites, are either destroyed or hopelessly scarred. Can we, in fact, change our natures? There is no answer in Wilder's conclusion—only a vague hope that something may be salvaged from our experience. A hope, not a promise.

There are some weaknesses in the novel. Sometimes the writing, particularly in the epilogue, is a little self-conscious; sometimes minor characters, like Mrs. Bernstein, the banker's wife, appear on the scene but contribute nothing to the action. Above all, Wilder's fondness for fantasy, to which he introduces us in the character of Virgil, does not blend easily with the realism of the story. (One is all the more appreciative of his skill in *Our Town* when he successfully fuses these two contrary elements.) Yet *The Cabala* holds a number of attractions. The best portrait is that of Alix, vivid in her humor, her wit, her grace of mind and spirit—and her agony. Equally memorable is Cardinal Vaini, who suggests a painting by Goya: he has a scope and a power we do not meet again until Julius Caesar in *The Ides of March*. Wilder tells us that none of the characters are based on real people such as he might have met when he was in Rome and about the same age as Samuele— twenty-six. On the contrary, they are entirely creatures of his fancy, derived from "reading matter and from day-dreaming, a bookworm's work." Possibly the only character modeled from life is Samuele himself: he is a more learned, more intellectual, more sophisticated, more polished George Brush, but essentially possessed of the same puritanical point of view and the same callowness. And Brush, by Wilder's own admission, is at least one-fourth the author's own personality.

From a historical standpoint *The Cabala* is memorable

in another way: it diagnoses with painful clarity the ills of Europe, a subject that American writers were little concerned with in the 1920's. For most of them the continent was a convenient backdrop against which Americans could play out their conflicts. The sickness it was suffering from was, understandably, more the province of its own authors, such as Franz Kafka or Thomas Mann. But from the first Wilder demonstrated a sympathy for, and an understanding of, Europe that his contemporaries did not share—perhaps one reason why he has always been so highly regarded abroad. Remote from America though its setting is, *The Cabala* has nothing escapist about it. Because of the way in which Wilder has drawn his characters we can perceive all too plainly what their future path is likely to be. Wrapped in the past, clinging to illusions, yearning for a glory gone forever, they will bend to the storm that the coming political charlatan raises and joyfully embrace his vision of a new Roman Empire. To become acquainted with the Cabalists is to understand the major cause of the fever called Fascism that raged through the Italian and the European aristocracy. Of course Wilder was making no predictions about the years that lay ahead in this book, but given such seeds, what else could the harvest bring?

Although *The Cabala* is set in modern Italy, its roots are in the past. For his next novel, *The Bridge of San Luis Rey,* which appeared the following year, Wilder chose another foreign land, Peru. And on this occasion he literally moved back in time—to the year 1714.

Like *The Cabala,* it is another example of the "bookworm's work," for Wilder drew upon several literary sources for his characters. The Marquesa de Monte-mayor is modeled after Mme. de Sévigué, the seven-teenth-century French writer who, through her letters, gave the world a glimpse of her brilliance and wit. The actress Camilla Perichole is a character taken from *La Carosse du Saint Sacré* by the nineteenth-century French novelist Prosper Mérimée. And the discussions in the book that center on such writers as Lope da Vega and Calderón reveal Wilder's knowledge of, and feeling for, the Spanish literature of the seventeenth century—its Golden Age. Even the structure of Wilder's book sug-gests an earlier novel—his own: Part One, which is a kind of prologue, is balanced by Part Five, the epilogue; and the chapters between, like those in *The Cabala,* also focus on three sets of characters. And finally, just as Samuele serves to tie the threads of *his* book together, so a narrator, following the career of Brother Juniper and his investigations, adds information for the reader's benefit in a kind of omniscient voice. The narrator is not, properly speaking, a character in the book: he is simply the auctorial "I."

The Bridge can most correctly be characterized as a Christian novel in that it deals with themes and ideas that are part of the Christian faith. For example, what might be regarded as failure in the eyes of the world may, in fact, be success in the judgment of God. Suffering, which so often seems pointless, may have a significance, although we apprehend it only "through a glass, darkly." Thus Part One is entitled "Perhaps an Accident"; Part Five, "Perhaps an Intention." What looks like happenstance may indeed have a design to it, but one cannot be sure; hence the "perhaps." As Wilder himself has explained it, it is the "magic unity of purpose and chance, destiny and accident, that I have tried to describe in my books."

Other traditional Christian themes abound. There is value in suffering as a means of transforming character and ennobling it. Not, it must be added, the passive kind that turns a human being into an unthinking slave, but rather the willingness to recognize that pain and death are threads in the tapestry of life. We cannot avoid them, but we can use them to enrich the pattern of our existence. To put it another way: shadows can obscure, but when used intelligently by an artist they can add depth and vividness to a canvas. But the artist in paint must be conscious of what he is doing. Correspondingly, those who are (or would be) artists in living must be aware that every act of theirs can be given meaning by their reaction to life's pressures, every experience that shapes them is a bead strung into the necklace of existence. Wilder stands midway between those writers of the past who accepted their religion more or less unquestioningly ("Whatever is, is right") and those of his own day who relegated faith to the junk-heap of superstition. Perhaps Arthur Koestler, in his novel *The Age of Longing,* summed up the problem best [the italics in the quotation have been added]:

Some people suffer and become saints. Others, by the same experience, are turned into brutes thirsting for vengeance. Others, just into neurotics. *To*

*draw spiritual nourishment from suffering, one must be
endowed with the right kind of digestive system.* Otherwise suffering turns sour on one. It was bad policy
on the part of God to inflict suffering indiscriminately. It was like ordering laxatives for every
kind of disease.

By and large, the people who most interest Wilder
and the characters he most favors in his books are those
with "the right kind of digestive system." Possibly it is his
concentration on this category of human being (as
contrasted, say, with such writers as François Mauriac or
Graham Greene, who focus on those who have turned
sour) that sometimes makes Wilder's philosophy seem
too Pollyana-ish and his work too bland. Certainly the
serenity of his point of view is in sharp conflict with the
kind of novel that was being written in 1927, an age
deeply preoccupied with the "lost generation."

If suffering, however, is to be seen in its positive
aspects, another element must accompany it: resignation, the acceptance of the will of God. Consequently,
although death comes to the leading characters of *The
Bridge* (in fact, death occupies the foreground of all
Wilder's novels and plays), suicide seldom makes its
appearance. For death belongs to the natural order of
things, whereas suicide, the final act of defiant despair,
disturbs the pattern. (Marcantonio of *The Cabala* is one
of the few who takes this route.) Although the characters have known despair that has brought them to the
brink of self-destruction, when death finds them on the
bridge they have overcome their agony and look forward to a new and better life. Having discovered the

noblest portion of their natures when they were under stress, they really have, artistically speaking, no further reason to survive. They have fulfilled their destiny.

Because so much of the novel deals with the theme of suffering, it necessarily explores its concomitant, loneliness. All the characters in *The Bridge* are, in one way or another, isolated: from God, from society, from relatives, from friends, from lovers. Even when they are most surrounded by groups of people, they are most conscious of their alienation. The Marquesa is abandoned by her daughter, whom she loves; Estaban and Manuel, twin brothers, are orphans who have neither family nor friends; Pepita, who dies with the Marquesa, is also alone in the world; and Uncle Pio and the little boy, Jaime, have little beyond each other. Like Christ, praying alone in the Garden of Gethsemane, forgotten by disciples who were too tired to keep watch with Him, those on the bridge live out their days forgotten by their fellows. But when they understand and accept the fact that loneliness is the natural condition (in the words of a character in T. S. Eliot's *The Cocktail Party*, "Hell is oneself, Hell is alone, the other figures in it merely projections. . . . One is always alone."), they begin to appreciate their common humanity. And at the same time they learn the name of the only cure for their loneliness—a love that transcends self.

Though Wilder, when he wrote this novel, was only thirty, he had already developed a technique that was going to prove increasingly useful in giving shape to his major ideas. In such widely divergent future novels as *Heaven's My Destination* and *The Ides of March,* in plays

like *Our Town* and *The Skin of Our Teeth,* he simply
refines what he is doing in *The Bridge.* The themes in
The Bridge are serious, transcendental. The content is
religious, philosophical. From a practical point of view,
these elements are not going to send the average reader
rushing to buy the book. So Wilder's style becomes
simple, unadorned; more important, he juxtaposes
theological problems with everyday activities. For example, he spends some time describing the bridge physically: how well it is built, of what it is made, how proud the
people are of its fame. It is quite important as a
utilitarian object. We are so lulled by the ordinary, it
seems so much part of our own lives, that we look no
further. And when we have become comfortable with its
familiar things, suddenly they turn into something else
and become metaphysical symbols. That is why *Our
Town,* which has a great deal to say about abstract
subjects, is so convincing in its concentration on detail.
And again, in *The Ides of March,* where Wilder raises
questions that go far beyond the world of Julius Caesar,
he surrounds these questions with the trivia of gossip,
domestic intrigue, all the petty considerations of our
daily routine had we been Romans. But this is not a
mere literary device that Wilder employs to popularize
his work: it springs from a belief that is characteristic of
his temperament. One's immortal soul and one's laundry *have* to be considered simultaneously.

Like *The Eighth Day,* written forty years later, *The
Bridge* opens with a calm recitation of a disaster—the
death of five people caused by the collapse of a bridge.
Significantly, the day on which it happens is Friday,

Passion Day; the time is exactly noon—both hands of the clock pointing up. The faceless narrator tells us that everyone is deeply upset by the tragedy, though he cannot understand why, since people have accepted all sorts of other misfortunes with equanimity: tidal waves, earthquakes, crumbling towers. But there was something different, something special about this bridge, and so a little Franciscan friar who "accidentally" happened to be in Peru at that time converting the Indians and who has witnessed the misfortune, decides to investigate the reason for it. It is Brother Juniper who initiates the first part, "Perhaps an Accident," for by discovering why those particular five people were the victims he believes he can prove that the universe operates according to a plan. Rather delightfully, Wilder gives us a brief sketch of the little Franciscan, who sees no reason why theology cannot be an exact science, like mathematics. In his own way he suggests George Brush of a later Wilder novel or Samuele of the earlier book: all three are do-gooders full of enthusiasm, vitality, idealism, and honor. And in a way all three take on hopeless tasks. Samuele tries to "save" the clearly damned Marcantonio; Brother Juniper intends to "prove" God exists; George Brush determines to "reform" the human race. That all these goals are unattainable never enters their heads: they remain true to the uniquely American tradition of *Excelsior!*

As he is described, Brother Juniper hardly seems an Italian Catholic: he sounds much more like Wilder's analysis of an American Protestant: "There is no limit to the degree with which an American is imbued with the doctrine of progress. Place and environment are but décor to his journey. . . . He is what he is because his plans characterize him." This evaluation, made by the author twenty-five years after *The Bridge* was written, is still correct. Despite the general corruption, the economic inequities, the political ignorance, and the military tragedies to be found in certain Asiatic countries, the simple act of getting the population to vote—whether or not it understands what it is doing—proves to many Americans that democracy is at work. (It was precisely this simplistic view of life that exasperated Charles Dickens a century before in *Martin Chuzzlewit.*) Few American writers, however severely they criticize their native land, do it as subtly, as gracefully, and as ironically as Wilder.

He has a little more fun with Brother Juniper in another capacity. Since the Franciscan looks upon it as his life's work to "justify the ways of God to man," he is forever keeping records, like a schoolteacher giving his students grades. He has, for instance, "a complete record of the Prayers for Rain and their results" (Americans are nothing if not pragmatists!). When the pestilence destroys a large number of peasants, he "secretly drew up a diagram of the characteristics of fifteen victims and fifteen survivors. . . . Each soul was rated upon a basis of ten as regards its goodness, its diligence in religious observance, and its importance to its family group." The only trouble is that after Brother Juniper finishes adding and subtracting and juggling his figures and statistics, he estimates "that the dead were five times more worth saving" than those who lived! He is badly shaken by the knowledge that "the discrepancy between faith and the facts is greater than is generally realized." George Brush is going to be shocked by the same discovery in *Heaven's My Destination*.

Yet while he has been busy collecting all the data about those who perished, Brother Juniper, a kind of eighteenth-century human computer, never really learns much about the five people he has studied. He gathers all the proper information, but what evades him is the central passion of their lives. At this point the narrator intrudes on the story and asks: "And I, who claim to know so much more, isn't it possible that even I have missed the very spring within the spring?" For the truth is, all human existence is a mystery, and no one can know everything about everyone. And even if one could, one could never understand the clockwork complications of the soul. The narrator concludes the first part:

> Some say that we shall never know and that to the gods we are like the flies that the boys kill on a summer day, and some say, on the contrary, that the very sparrows do not lose a feather that has not been brushed away by the finger of God.

Interestingly enough, *The Eighth Day* concludes with much the same observation:

> There is much talk of a design in the arras. Some are certain they see it. Some see what they have been told to see. Some remember that they saw it once but have lost it. Some are strengthened by seeing a pattern wherein the oppressed and exploited of the

earth are gradually emerging from their bondage. Some find strength in the conviction that there is nothing to see. Some

and the sentence is left hanging for others to fill in as the river of life flows on.

The next three parts of *The Bridge* take up the lives of the people who were killed. The Marquesa de Montemayor, a middle-aged woman who has made an unhappy marriage, turns to her daughter, Doña Clara, as a substitute for her lost emotional life and pours all her love out on the girl. Doña Clara, like James Blair in *The Cabala,* is a frigid young person with no love to give; further, she despises her mother's excessive demonstrations of affection. As quickly as she can she marries a Spanish grandee and returns with him to his home in Spain, leaving her mother in Peru. The Marquesa has only one outlet for her feelings: she turns to writing letters to her daughter as a means of binding them together, for literature "is the notation of the heart." The most trivial details transform themselves into lofty thoughts through the magic of the Marquesa's imagination: like the nineteenth-century German poet Heinrich Heine, out of her great suffering she makes little songs. Without her realizing it, her agony has come to have some meaning.

Meanwhile she continues writing her lovely, graceful letters, but as her daughter seldom answers her she begins to drink. Finally she becomes a public spectacle because of the scenes she makes, so that when she attends the theater an actress performing there mimics her and provokes the laughter of the audience. The actress is La Perichole, and it is she who provides the link with the other characters on the bridge, moving in and out of their lives like a brightly colored thread.

Because of the Marquesa's loneliness the Abbess Madre Maria del Pilar sends a young girl, Pepita, to keep her company. Pepita loves the Abbess, suffers at leaving the convent, is unhappy with the Marquesa, and longs to return. She goes so far as to write a letter to the Abbess begging that she be allowed to come back—but she never sends the letter, for she knows that the best proof she can give the Abbess of her love is to do as she is bidden. In Pepita's love there is both self-discipline and self-sacrifice. The Marquesa, coming upon the letter "accidentally," understands for the first time how selfish her love for her daugher had been, how strong an element there was of a wish to dominate, to impress. Had she, in fact, ever really looked at her daughter as a person? Or had her daughter merely served as a mirror for her own needs and desires? In the words of William Blake, the Marquesa has sought "only Self to please/To bind another to Its delight," while Pepita knows that "Love seeketh not Itself to please. . . . But for another gives its ease."

The evening before Pepita and the Marquesa cross the bridge to return to Lima, the old woman looks out at the starry night—such a night as Samuele observed when his ship sailed for home. For both the Marquesa and Samuele there has been a small epiphany; for both, life now has some meaning. And as the Marquesa raises her eyes to the heavens, she whispers, "Let me live now . . . let me begin again."

It is, of course, too late. As a character in *Our Town* observes, "We never make the most of our opportunities." But the Marquesa has had her moment of illumination—her moment of truth, to borrow from the language of the bullfight. And who is to say that it is worth nothing because it is so short?

The next section concerns the twin brothers Esteban and Manuel, who were abandoned as babies at the convent run by the Abbess. As they grow up they become more and more isolated from the world, more and more dependent on each other. They even have the knack of anticipating each other's wishes and wants without the need for speech. Between them there exists the bond that is lacking between the Marquesa and her daughter. But while the Marquesa is gradually moving in the direction of unselfish love, the love between the brothers, already too extreme, is tarnished by the intrusion of La Perichole, who arouses the passion of both brothers and for the first time awakens jealousy in their breasts.

Though Manuel and Estaban sincerely love each other, it is Manuel who feels more deeply. Recognizing that Estaban is suffering (La Perichole favors Manuel largely because he is a scribe who writes letters for her), Manuel gives her up. Before long he has an accident, contracts a fever from an infected foot, and in his delirium cries out his love for La Perichole. Although Estaban has profited from his brother's sacrificial gesture of renunciation, he is plagued by guilt; when Manuel dies Estaban's collapse is so total that he refuses to be himself any longer and pretends that he is Manuel. Only in this way can he keep his brother alive. He drifts aimlessly, making the acquaintance of a Captain Alvarado; decides to accompany the captain on his ship, changes his mind, contemplates suicide, and is prevented from this act by the Captain, also grieving for someone he has loved and lost. The Captain reminds him that "We push on, as best we can." Estaban's moment of illumination comes when he realizes that self-destruction is not the answer. And at that moment of grace he crosses the bridge. The Captain, who has had to supervise the passage of merchandise, does not pass over at the same time, and so he lives. But he is an unhappy man. And though he dies, Estaban is a happy one in that he obtained his wish—but not by his own hand.

The last section dealing with the other two victims is perhaps the least interesting, partly because of the characters, partly because Wilder has already made his point clearly enough and here simply repeats himself. Uncle Pio, alone in the world, has taken La Perichole into his profession and made a great actress out of her. She is a coarse, ignorant, vulgar woman; love, for her, is defined exclusively through sex. After a successful stage career and an interlude as the Viceroy's mistress, by whom she has three children, she leaves the stage. At the same time she suddenly discovers a craving for virtue and becomes more pious and proper than the most dedicated churchwoman. Finally she wearies of even this pose and embarks on a series of futile, furtive affairs.

Over the years Uncle Pio has learned something from his life and his amours: he never again "regarded any human being, from a prince to a servant, as a mechanical object." But not so Camilla, La Perichole. When he tells her of his devotion and wishes they could go away to some island where "the people would know [her] and love [her] for" herself, she laughs at him. "There is no such thing as that kind of love and that kind of island. It's in the theatre you find such things." La Perichole has never known real love. But she *has* known real art. And that, too, is a bridge.

Camilla and Uncle Pio drift apart until he discovers, again "accidentally," that she has been stricken with smallpox, and although she survives the disease, she loses all her beauty, of which she had been so vain. With its passing she knows that love will also die, for she had never been able to separate her beauty from the responses it evoked in her admirers: who could love her now that she was ugly and disfigured? And here the narrator interrupts to define the limitations of passion:

> . . . though it expends itself in generosity and thoughtfulness, though it give birth to visions and to great poetry, [it] remains among the sharpest expressions of self-interest. Not until it has passed through a long servitude, through its own self-hatred, through mockery, through great doubts, can it take its place among the loyalties.

Uncle Pio, recognizing Camilla's complete spiritual shipwreck and anxious to salvage her little boy, Jaime, pleads with her to give the boy to him for a year. He loves Jaime, he wants to teach him, to raise him. And for the first time Camilla has an unselfish emotion: she consents to give the child up for his own good. Jaime will make a fresh start, Uncle Pio can renew himself in the boy, the future seems bright. As they draw near the bridge Uncle Pio tells Jaime that when they cross it "they would sit down and rest, but it turned out not to be necessary."

At the end of the novel Brother Juniper, having amassed all the necessary facts, which only baffle him since the key to the puzzle is missing, writes his book. The inferences he draws are confusing. Pepita was a good child, so was Jaime. Therefore the accident called the young to Heaven while they were still pure. On the other hand, Uncle Pio had led a dissolute life and the Marquesa was an avaricious drunkard. Therefore the accident punished the wicked. But how could the same accident perform two such different functions? In the midst of the friar's bafflement his book catches the eye of certain judges, who decide poor Brother Juniper is guilty of heresy because he has presumed to explain God's plan. As he sits in his cell awaiting punishment in the flames, he ponders over the riddle, anxious to find some meaning in his own demise, which would not be unwelcome if it brought some illumination. But he never finds the answer he is seeking; he simply calls upon St. Francis (feeling too inferior to invoke God at the moment of death), and leans upon a flame and dies, smiling.

The funeral of the victims on the bridge brings together all those who were left behind. The Marquesa's daughter visits the Abbess, showing her mother's last

letter and her transformation. La Perichole visits the
Abbess and tells her of Estaban, Pepita, Uncle Pio, and
Jaime. Before their deaths the five characters had, in
Catholic terms, entered a state of grace, and by their
deaths they have transformed those whom they loved. It
does not matter that in a little while no one will
remember them. For the Abbess knows:

> . . . soon we shall die and all memory of those
> five will have left the earth, and we ourselves
> shall be loved for a while and forgotten. But the
> love will have been enough; all those impulses of
> love return to the love that made them. Even
> memory is not necessary for love. There is a land
> of the living and a land of the dead and the
> bridge is love, the only surivival, the only mean-
> ing.

Every type of love is scrutinized in this novel: primi-
tive sexual love, exaggerated fraternal love, one-sided
mother love. All are, in one way or another, impure.
But all pass through a kind of filter that drains off the
dross, and what is left is the Christian *agape*—people
loving each other in the same way God loves them. How
deep this longing is in the human race may be seen
today: despite its distortion, confusion, debasement, the
cry to "make love, not war," the "love-ins" of the flower
children, the renunciation of possessions, of "things,"
are a pathetic echo, a shadow of the substance that
people seek, even if unknowingly.

So, although Brother Juniper did not prove to his
satisfaction that there was any design in the fall of the

bridge, or in the deaths of the five who were present, those who read the book know that there was a meaning in these events, after all. By laying the story before us, the narrator enables us to see further than Brother Juniper, even as God, the Narrator, can see beyond us. It is safe to say that those with religious beliefs feel buttressed by *The Bridge of San Luis Rey;* those without them remain politely skeptical. For this is the final lesson of the novel: that faith has nothing to do with reason. If Brother Juniper had accepted instead of trying to prove, he would never have needed to write his book. And so need never have died.

It makes small sense, then, to quarrel with the book's theology, as some critics have done, a few arguing that every incident tries so hard to pile up proof of the "intention" that the book collapses, like the bridge, under such an artificial weight of evidence. Nor is there much point in arguing that Wilder ought to have confined himself to a world he knew instead of retreating to eighteenth-century Lima, where he had never even been in the twentieth century! One might as well censure Emily Brontë for presuming to write a love story like *Wuthering Heights* when it was entirely outside her experience. The artist must take his material how and where he can: what is important is the successful creation of the world he invites us to enter. On its own terms *The Bridge* works; its very timelessness, its suspension in space, may in fact allow it to endure longer than other works of a different cast published during the same period—for example, the once-relevant, newspaperlike novels of John Dos Passos. It is almost as though Wilder had examined the exiles inhabiting the universe of Ernest Hemingway's *The Sun Also Rises,* the idle and the sybaritic who waft through F. Scott Fitzgerald's *The Great Gatsby,* the poor and the outcast who populate Sidney Kingsley's *Dead End,* and said, "Yes, there is death; yes, there is boredom; yes, there is poverty and despair. But are you quite sure there is nothing else?" While most American writers of the time were busy showing the reading public an earth cut off from the light by a moral or economic eclipse, Wilder was gently reminding us that the sun was still there and that the darkness would have to pass for the simple reason that Nature had so ordained it. *The Bridge of San Luis Rey* remains a tribute to its author's particular vision, his uncompromising integrity as an artist, and—a peculiarly American virtue—his rugged individualism.

The next few years, from 1927 to 1930, were Wilder's fallow period. He published *The Angel That Troubled the Waters* in 1928, though most of the playlets in the volume had been written long before, indicating that he was now seriously moving toward another art form— the stage. And it was also during this time that he and his sister wandered through Europe studying the continental theaters, which had a far stronger influence on Wilder than on other American playwrights.

In 1930 his next novel, *The Woman of Andros,* appeared. Although it was based on a comedy by the Roman playwright Terence, in reality it owed nothing to the earlier work in either tone or philosophy. Terence's *Andria* was little more than a slapstick farce (what we might today describe as a "situation comedy"), including conflicts between parents and children; a boy-meets-girl, boy-loses-girl, boy-gets-girl formula; a lowly born ingenue who proves to be the long-lost daughter of a well-born father; and, a staple of classical comedy, an intriguing slave who is wiser than his master. Terence's play seems to have been an excuse for Wilder to use antiquity as his setting rather than the basis of inspiration for his novel.

Briefly, Terence tells the story of Glycerium (the girl from Andros), whose sister, Chrysis, is a courtesan. A young Roman of good family, Pamphilus, falls in love with Glycerium, although his father, Simo, disapproves because of the girl's family—or lack of it. However, when Glycerium becomes pregnant, Pamphilus determines to marry her, despite his father's objections. But there really is no problem after all, for Glycerium is not, as everyone supposed, the sister of a courtesan but the missing and supposedly dead daughter of a gentleman who is Simo's best friend. She is, in short, the equal in rank of the young man who loves her. (We sometimes forget that although Cinderella sat by the ashes and was badly treated, she was also the daughter of a nobleman: the Prince was not stooping that much when he married her.) At first glance it seems hard to imagine what there could have been in this tale to interest Wilder. But the imagination of a writer can give shape to the most unlikely material, even as a glass-blower using the heat of the furnace can change the form of the object with which he is working.

To begin with, there are no designing slaves in Wilder's novel to supply comic relief or help unravel the plot. Next, Glycerium is not proven to be a girl of good family, as she was in Terence's play, but is indeed Chrysis's sister; therefore the young man is faced with the genuine problem of marrying someone outside of his class and so alienating his father. Terence's play ends with wedding bells and a child newly born to the happy couple, but in Wilder's novel Glycerium dies, adding to the somber note of the book. But perhaps the most interesting shift is in the choice of the major character: although we do not see Glycerium in Terence's comedy, she occupies the center of the action. In *The Woman of Andros* the spotlight is on her sister, Chrysis. And in the portrait of Chrysis Wilder reveals the purpose of his book.

As he limns her, she is a sensitive, educated young woman, deeply versed in the teachings of Socrates, fond of the plays of Euripides, whom she favors above the other playwrights, devoted to her sister, remote from the people among whom she lives. (Like the characters of Wilder's other novels, she, too, is alone.) The dwellers on the island of Brynos (Terence had used Athens for his locale) distrust her because she is "different" from them: she knows too much, she looks at life from her own point of view and is unwilling to accept conventional interpretations; above all, they disapprove of her improper way of life. Yet she conducts herself in a manner seldom associated with the profession of courtesan: she feeds the hungry, helps the homeless, tends the sick. Her hearth is always open to the human strays who have been battered by life's storms. In many ways she suggests Alix of *The Cabala.*

Chrysis, who is thirty-five when the book begins, meets the twenty-five-year-old Pamphilus during festivities in her home. They have been reading the prayer that marks the end of *The Phaedrus:* "Grant that I may become beautiful in the inner man and may whatever I possess without be in harmony with that which is within." They look at each other, suddenly conscious of a bond between them, and they fall in love. The bond is intellectual and spiritual as much as physical, for Pamphilus is also different from the others. He has read more than the other young men, he is more perceptive, he is infinitely kinder. Though she is happy with him, Chrysis is aware that her love is greater than his (again the old Wilder theme of *il y a toujours un qui baise et l'autre qui tourne la joue*—"there is always one who loves and one who lets himself be loved"), and she recognizes too that "the most difficult burden is the incommunicability of love." Still they are happy together, although Simo, the father of Pamphilus, wishes him to settle down with a bride the old man has chosen for his son: Philumene, the daughter of Simo's friend Chremes.

Because of her deep affection for her fifteen-year-old sister, Glycerium, Chrysis has kept the girl away from the prying eyes of the world, determined to protect her from cruelty and loss of innocence as long as possible. But one day, when Glycerium ventures out, she is jeered at by some young men who threaten her; it is Pamphilus who comes to her rescue and with whom she falls in love. He responds to her, even though he is fond of Chrysis: as he watches Glycerium along the shore at their first meeting he is moved by the fragility, the beauty, the transience of the moment, which is at once lovely and poignant, recalling Stephen Dedalus' first sight of the young, unknown girl on the beach in James Joyce's *Portrait of the Artist.* Pamphilus is torn between his feeling for both sisters, but Chrysis, who is wiser (as well as older) than he, recognizes that his love for Glycerium is natural and right. Like the elegant and worldly Marschallin of Richard Strauss' opera *Der Rosenkavalier,* Chrysis gives her blessing to Glycerium and Pamphilus, knowing that they will be happy with each other. Pamphilus still struggles with his concepts of right and wrong, good and bad: it is Chrysis who reminds him that "of all the forms of genius, goodness has the longest awkward age." (Wilder, incidentally, is to use this aphorism as the center of his next novel, *Heaven's My Destination.*) On the whole, it is Chrysis who gives the book its flavor of understanding and tolerance.

This sense of forgiveness and charity extends to the character of Pamphilus' father, Simo. Although he is anxious for his son to make the "right" kind of marriage, unlike the parental tyrants of Roman comedy he appreciates his boy's dilemma and does not press him to follow the expected pattern. On the contrary, it is Pamphilus' mother, Sostrata, who provides whatever opposition exists. It is not only that she resents her son's interest in a girl who is beneath him; he is guilty, philosophically speaking, of something far worse: he is daring to be different in the choice he makes. For Sostrata "Society *was* similarity," and Pamphilus' refusal to conform makes him dangerous. The character of Sostrata seems an indirect comment on Wilder's own conviction that an individual must be allowed the freedom to be himself.

Glycerium, now pregnant, becomes a responsibility for Pamphilus that he must meet, despite his mother's objections. Simo, respecting his son's wishes, defers, much to Sostrata's irritation. But by now Chrysis has fallen ill—fatally; and as she lies in bed she is filled with terror, not at the thought of death but at its ugliness: she fears that she may leave the world "with cries of pain, with a torn mind, and with discomposed features." In this most solemn of moments she and Pamphilus can utter only trivial sentences, both too much moved by the immensity of the experience to be able to express themselves adequately. But before she dies she tells him what she really believes:

> I want to say to someone . . . that I have known the worst that the world can do to me, and that nevertheless I praise the world and all living. All that is, is well. Remember some day, remember me as one who loved all things and accepted from the gods all things, the bright and the dark.

At Chrysis' funeral Glycerium throws herself on her sister's body; when Pamphilus helps her up Simo realizes that his son must be allowed to make his own choice of a wife. Afraid that Glycerium is too frail to bear strong sons, he nevertheless accepts her as his future daughter-in-law. He remembers one of Chrysis' aphorisms: "The mistakes we make through generosity are less terrible than the gains we acquire through caution."

To help himself resolve his problem, Pamphilus turns

to fasting. He does not understand life, he does not comprehend the necessity of Chrysis' death, he has no clear picture of his own future. Meanwhile, the death of Chrysis has brought sharp changes to the household: everyone in it, including her sister, will be sold as slaves. In pity for Glycerium's condition and out of love for his son, Simo buys the girl so that Pamphilus will be able to marry her. But Glycerium dies in childbirth, and with her the baby. What, then, has been the meaning behind all these tragic events?

Since it is a fundamental belief in Wilder's canon that everything has a meaning—*if* we choose to give it one—the answer is to be found at the end of the novel. During the course of the story the island has suffered from a drought; now the rain begins to fall. As the book begins with a description of the island at night—dark— so it concludes with another night scene, studded with stars (the same symbolism of *The Cabala* and *The Bridge of San Luis Rey*). But there is an even deeper significance, for the book is set in pagan times, before the coming of Christianity. Yet now the moon shines down, and "in the East the stars shone tranquilly down upon the land that was soon to be called Holy and that even then was preparing its precious burden." (The last words of the novel repeat the sentence that opens it, giving a kind of circular effect to the whole.) The novel, in short, prefigures the birth of Christ.

Chrysis, as we have seen, is unlike her neighbors. She embodies the best of the classical tradition, uniting an appreciation of this life with a craving for something beyond it, although she is not sure of what she is seeking. She spends long hours poring over books, hoping to find the answer. But because her world has not yet seen the coming of Christ, she lacks the key to everything, for it is Christian theology that suggests the meaning of suffering, the significance of life, the concept of immortality. She is like someone shut away from a vision perceived intuitively; in her wonder and her longing she might well say, like Shakespeare's Caliban:

> Sometimes a thousand twangling instruments
> Will hum about mine ears; and sometimes voices,
> That, if I then had wak'd after long sleep,
> Will make me sleep again; and then, in dreaming,
> The clouds methought would open and show
> riches
> Ready to drop upon me, that, when I wak'd,
> I cried to dream again.

It is not enough, then, to be a humanist: that is only half the story. The combination of Christian faith with classical humanism is what makes the perfect whole. Chrysis perhaps perceives it when she is dying: her acceptance of "the bright and the dark" certainly suggests Christian resignation. And the minor characters mirror the same idea. Pamphilus' sister, Argo, for instance, is suffering from an earache that is finally cured because "there is one thing greater than curing a malady and that is accepting a malady and sharing its acceptance." (Strictly speaking, Wilder has taken this last statement from a nineteenth-century French philosopher, but it nevertheless belongs in the context of what he is saying.) And another minor character, a half-insane sea captain whom Chrysis has supported out of

charity, also realizes that when he abandons self and
begins to consider others, when he recognizes that
greed and offended pride blind people to the truth,
when he turns his back on the folly of worldly success—
then he can begin to live. We must die to ourselves in
order to be born in Christ. And so, if the world of *The
Woman of Andros* is pagan, clearly the longing—and the
perception—is Christian. Like the characters in *The
Bridge of San Luis Rey,* who have their epiphany before
the bridge collapses, Chrysis travels as far as it is possible
for her to go along the road to self-knowledge; when
she reaches the end, she, too, dies.

In contrast to Chrysis, the people on the island are
not interested in anything much beyond material possessions. (Wilder here may have been indirectly commenting on a subject treated quite frequently by his
fellow-American writers in the 1920's and 1930's: Sinclair Lewis' *Babbitt* and Eugene O'Neill's *Marco's Millions*
have much to say about American acquisitiveness.)
They remain outside the circle of her radiance. One
reason, indeed, why Wilder might have chosen Brynos
for his setting rather than Athens, as in the original
play, is that he was trying to dramatize the plight of a
people cut adrift from the culture and the civilization
that Athens represented. At the same time, Brynos is an
important shrine, for it involves the legendary figure of
Aesculapius, the patron saint of medicine, and his
father, Apollo, the god of poetry, prophecy, and healing. The island, then, like the one in *The Tempest,* has a
magic of its own, but most of the people living on it are
unaware of what it symbolizes.

Pamphilus is thus the perfect link between the inhabitants and Chrysis: his mother, Sostrata, belongs with the world of greed and conformity; his father, Simo, has a vision of something better; it is left to Pamphilus to ask Chrysis to resolve a feeling she thinks is merely "one of the meaningless accesses of despair that descend upon adolescence when the slow ache of existence is first apprehended by the growing mind." In turn Chrysis tells the story of a hero who in a vision was allowed to revisit the earth and "to live over again that day in all the twenty-two thousand days of his life-time that had been least eventful; but it must be with a mind divided into two persons—the participant and the onlooker: the participant who does the deeds and says the words of so many years before and the onlooker who foresees the end." The hero cannot bear to do this, for he begins to see with agonizing clarity how aimlessly people live, wasting their precious moments, unconscious of the swift passage of time, unable to shape their acts into something significant and enduring. And so he pleads to be allowed to return to reality. Years later, Wilder was to dramatize this scene in *Our Town,* when Emily revisits Grover's Corners after her death.

As the novel progresses, Chrysis takes one step after another into a world of growing awareness. If she tries to teach Pamphilus or to answer his questions, at the same time she, too, is learning (which is always a byproduct of good teaching, anyway). In the end Chrysis reaches the level of understanding attained by the young priest of Aesculapius (he speaks no word throughout the entire novel but, Christlike, ministers to the sick and needy), and is able to express her belief that one day humanity will know why it is suffering: "Perhaps we shall meet somewhere beyond life when all these pains shall have been removed. I think the gods have some mystery still in store for us." The passage is an interesting parallel with one written by Chekhov in *The Three Sisters.* Their world is a Christian one, but their lives, too, seem to have no meaning. Olga cries:

> Time will pass, and we shall go away forever, and we shall be forgotten, our faces will be forgotten, our voices, and how many there were of us; but our sufferings will pass into joy for those who will live after us, happiness and peace will be established on earth, and they will remember kindly and bless those who have lived before . . . it seems as though a little more and we shall know what we are living for, why we are suffering . . . .

Wilder has admirably adapted his style here to the elegaic subject of the novel; the critic Malcolm Cowley aptly describes it as a Greek pastoral, a kind of long prose poem. The pace is much slower than in the previous novels, the tone more subdued. The sentence structure suggests that of *The Angel That Troubled the Waters,* more elaborate and rather consciously beautiful. Nevertheless, it does represent a drop from the standards of his earlier books, despite its several virtues.

Whatever tensions and conflicts can be found in the story are for the most part philosophical and abstract. That is, the characters, for all their attractions, remain symbols rather than people. The confrontations are little more than discussions carried on by agreeable, intelligent, well-intentioned human beings. There is much talk of pain and anguish, but very small indication of it. When one contrasts *The Woman of Andros* with *The Bridge of San Luis Rey* or even *The Cabala,* one sees how much less successful it is. All the same it is a valuable clue to Wilder's progress as a writer, even though it is less skillful in execution, for it defines several ideas that he is to pursue more successfully in later works. *The Woman of Andros* should be regarded as the rest in a musical composition: it was necessary for Wilder to write it in order to get on with the next melody.

Understandably, when critics review a book, particularly when the author is still young, they cannot be expected to examine the work in the light of his entire output, which is still in the future anyway. And perhaps it is only human nature that, having exalted Wilder's previous novel, *The Bridge of San Luis Rey,* they now derived some satisfaction from tearing *The Woman of Andros* to shreds. What genuinely enraged some critics, among them the Communist Michael Gold, was the escapist-like quality of the book. After all, it was 1930; America was living through the depression—a disaster of staggering proportions. What right had *any* artist to produce a book filled with a "daydream of homosexual figures in graceful gowns moving archaically among the lilies"? Labeling Wilder the "Prophet of the Genteel Christ," Gold insisted that the religion of the book was "Anglo-Catholicism, that last refuge of the American snob . . . that newly fashionable literary religion that

centers around Jesus Christ and the first British Gentleman." And Gold concluded his harangue:

> Is this the speech of a pioneer continent? Will this
> discreet French drawing-room hold all the blood,
> horror and hope of the world's new empire? . . .
> Where are the cotton mills . . . ? Where are
> the child slaves of the beet fields? Where are the
> stockbroker suicides, the labor racketeers, or pas-
> sion and death of the coal miners? . . . Is Mr.
> Wilder a Swede or a Greek, or is he an American?
> No stranger would know from these books he has
> written.

The rage Gold expressed was probably not entirely
political: it stirred up enough critics and readers to keep
letters circulating in newspapers and magazines for a
number of weeks, all expressing opinions either violently pro or con. The editors of *The New Republic*
finally refused to print any more correspondence on the
subject, being thoroughly tired of the controversy by
then.

In retrospect, the onslaught on Wilder seems amusing enough, the intemperate language of Gold absurd
rather than impressive. Like most politically oriented
critics, Gold could not accept a book as a work of art
unless it was (shades of the 1970's!) "relevant," exactly as
the Moscow critics called a 1940 production of Oscar
Wilde's *The Importance of Being Earnest* a perfect example of "corrupt, capitalistic society." (Even Shaw, in
1895, allowed his social conscience to run away with his

usual good sense as a critic and labeled Wilde's comedy "heartless.") It probably is just as pointless to demand that a work of art have relevance to the immediate political or social or economic situation as it is to question the utilitarian value of a rose. Even though *The Woman of Andros* missed as a work of art (that is, in its structure), there was no reason to debase its message or its author's purpose.

Precisely because America *was,* at that moment, in crisis, Wilder was trying to say something about the subjects that mattered in the world—the concerns beyond immediate possessions, just as today the so-called hippie culture is also dramatizing its views about the failure of "things" to give life meaning. Quite apart from Gold's application of the worker's interpretation of history to Wilder's novels, quite apart from his antipathy to tradition when revolution was its enemy, Gold reflected a certain pattern in America: the assumption that if people had elegance, breeding, or a sense of style they were therefore artificial and unreal. It is the same assumption that carries over into American political life: when the candidate for office shakes enough hands, kisses enough babies, looks enough of his constituents straight in the eye as a sign of complete candor (all this preferably with his jacket removed), he is therefore "sincere," a man of the people, "a regular guy." (It might be remembered that not so many years ago Adlai Stevenson's campaign managers worried about his literary style as being too "high-class for the voters.") As a result, Europe treated *The Woman of Andros* with a good deal more charity than America had;

while the continental critics were not blind to the faults of the novel they did not regard it as somehow un-American.

But the hue and cry had perhaps even more importance for Wilder's own career. How he felt after these attacks is not known: he had too much natural dignity to try to defend himself, as so many writers do after critical assaults. Still he must have thought deeply about the charges leveled against him, for in an interview eight years later he admitted:

> "For years I shrank from describing the modern world. I was alarmed at finding a way of casting into generalization the world of doorbells and telephones. . . . Now, though many of the subjects will often be of the past, I like to feel that I accept the twentieth century, not only as a fascinating age to live in, but as assimilable stuff to think with."

Certainly he was not again to produce as self-conscious and sentimental a book as *The Woman of Andros.* During the years from 1931 to 1938 his subjects are all (except for a translation) American in background, spare and simple in style, innovative in technique. And uniquely his own.

4 THE WEFT THREADS:
Time Present

One of the most persistent specters that haunts a writer is his fear of going stale: to the end of his life Charles Dickens was hounded by the thought that his inspiration might dry up—and with it his income. The twentieth-century writer suffers from a more exaggerated form of the same disease: over-photographed, over-interviewed, over-quoted, pressured to reveal the subject matter or even the title of his next book before the critical ink has been spilled over his last one; understandably concerned with his rating on the best-seller list (which often affects the sale of his novel or play to the films); driven to produce not only because of the need to express himself as an artist but also to prove, perhaps unconsciously, to a publicity-oriented world that he is still a name to be reckoned with, for nothing can be more obsolescent than last year's reputation—all

these considerations force an author to some kind of
self-examination after he has achieved his first real
success. How much truer this is when, two years after he
has climbed to the top of the literary tree he is toppled
by the arrows of critical displeasure. As we have seen,
the charges of reviewers like Michael Gold forced
Wilder to an evaluation of this phase of his career and,
in many ways, changed it. Two other forces certainly
combined to direct his efforts in another direction, and,
as always with Wilder, they came in the form of new
ideas. It is true that every writer is more or less
susceptible to the currents of his times, but it is not until
Wilder has thoroughly absorbed a concept, has apprehended it intellectually rather than emotionally, that
it can have any effect on his work.

Wilder's two-year visit to Europe and his study of its
theaters served him well in several ways. As he was
beginning to think seriously about writing for the stage
and had clearly indicated in all his own work, whether
fiction or drama, that he was not interested in realism as
a means of expression, he was forced to consider what
approach he might take so that he could give his ideas
their proper setting. In the late 1920's—and, indeed,
even before that—Europe had abandoned the realism
that had swept across the literary scene nearly three-
quarters of a century before and was experimenting
with novel techniques. Wilder was to derive inspiration
from them, since they meshed neatly with his own
notions: what he had to learn was to adapt the methods
to his own needs.

It was probably also an excellent idea for him to put

distance between himself and his native land: people and situations can often be seen more clearly when not viewed at close range. If Hemingway preferred to see a place before he wrote about it, Wilder appeared to deal with it more effectively after he had left and then returned to it. When, in 1931, he published his first volume of short plays, the themes of which were completely American, he was obviously looking at his country with fresh eyes.

Finally, and perhaps most important of all, the next five years, which attached him to the University of Chicago, plunged him into a kind of world—both academic and social—that he had not known before; and from that intellectual experience he was able to draw enough material to occupy him until the outbreak of World War II.

Just as Jean-Paul Sartre was to influence Wilder's thinking in later years, Gertrude Stein at this time contributed a great deal to his search for the right techniques. Of course, *what* a writer says ultimately dictates the form he chooses: it is not really possible to separate style from content. But when the artist is as tradition-conscious as Wilder, when he is always looking for a design that will impose some kind of order on chaos, it is safe to assume that he will be deeply interested in any concepts that can help him realize his goals. Gertrude Stein's theories, as the correspondence between them indicates, made enough of an impression on Wilder to cause him to translate them into his own terms.

That he was beginning himself to move in the direction of a discovery that would culminate in *Our Town* is apparent when we consider his first book of this second period. *The Long Christmas Dinner,* published in 1931, was a collection of six short plays, all of them worthy of being staged (unlike those in *The Angel That Troubled the Waters*) and largely American in theme. In addition, one element that had marred *The Cabala,* the uneasy marriage between fantasy and reality, was less troublesome in this volume, for Wilder had by now learned how to handle the mixture.

Three of the plays in the volume might be described as conventional in technique. "Queens of France," which is set in the New Orleans of 1869, is essentially the story of a confidence man, a lawyer, who encourages lonely women to offer proof of their royal birth so that they can claim the title of Queen of France. One of his clients is a spinster schoolteacher, one a housewife, one a cocotte. Although their lives are totally different in every way, they all become willing victims of the lawyer's game because the excitement of proving that they are really glamorous, beautiful people gives their lives some color. As the play ends the lawyer is busily fleecing still another "royal" client; the irony is, their lives would not be so drab, they would not need this artificially created excitement if they would realize that the simple state of being alive has a wonder all its own. If, as Thoreau maintained, "most men lead lives of quiet desperation," it is because, as Wilder sees it, they don't appreciate the magic of human existence. In *Our Town* Emily is to enlarge on this idea in a poignant speech after she is dead.

"Love and How to Cure It" has a London background: Soho, in 1895. A young undergraduate is in
love with a music-hall dancer, who rejects him. Breaking into the theater, Arthur Warburton flourishes a gun
at Linda, threatening to shoot her if she will not marry
him. But Joey, the comedian, slyly empties the gun and
makes it clear to Arthur that people who go around
shooting others for love really only love themselves. At
that moment the young man understands that Linda has
never been touched by passion. She is interested only in
her dancing. As with James Blair of *The Cabala,* love
is—and perhaps always will be, because of her nature—
beyond her experience.

A far better play than these two, although Wilder
thought poorly enough of it to drop it from the re-
printed volume, is "Such Things Only Happen in Books."
It is a variation on the idea in "Queens of France"—that
people dismiss details because they do not appreciate
their rich contribution to life—but it is told in a way that
suggests Wilder was, at the same time, poking gentle
fun at himself. John, a young novelist, lives in a quiet
New Hampshire village with his wife, Gabrielle. (In this
play the time is the present.) When the curtain goes up
they present a picture of domestic bliss: they are both
sitting in the library of their home, John playing solitaire, Gabrielle sewing. John is convinced that in life
"most people live along without plots. In fiction (like
cards) you have to adjust the cards to make a plot." On
the whole, books are seen as "a quiet, harmless fraud
about life." But as the play progresses, all sorts of
strange information can be gleaned. The servant, Katie,

has been tended by a doctor after she poured boiling water on herself by accident while she was washing her brother's clothes. As it turns out, her brother is a criminal she has been hiding in that very house for the past three months. Other details come to light—including the fact that John's devoted wife is the mistress of the doctor. But John is aware of none of this. When his wife mischievously points out that he is growing careless in his game of solitaire, he observes petulantly, "I certainly see all the moves that are to be seen. You don't expect me to look under the cards, do you?" John is as blind to the events of his surroundings as the powder-room attendant of Katherine Brush's short story, "Night Club": while horrendous crises are disrupting the lives of the women who wander in and out of the powder-room, Mrs. Brady is too busy reading *True Story* and *True Romances* to appreciate what is happening. Having eyes, they see not; having ears, they hear not. And they, too, miss the wonder of the human experience.

But it is with the characterization and the dramatic effectiveness that Wilder achieves a creditable growth. If the characters are not memorable, they are at least believable. And the practical demands of the theater are met in these plays, too: they are not so amorphous or philosophical as to evaporate when the curtain rises. Best of all, the dialogue is quite different from Wilder's earlier efforts: it *sounds* like the language of ordinary, everyday people. And it is speakable—actable. Yet what makes this volume impressive is the treatment he accords the three remaining plays.

"The Long Christmas Dinner," which gives the collection its name, is a study in one of Wilder's favorite subjects—obsessions, if you will—time. In an article written some twenty years later, Wilder was to relate this preoccupation to America itself. After noting that the European is what he is because he is familiar with the "immemorial repetitions of [his] country's way of life" as it surrounds him, Wilder adds, "An American can have no such stabilizing relation to any one place, nor to any one community, nor to any one moment in time."

Whether because of its size, geographical position, historical antecedents, or technological skill, this country, when compared with older civilizations, has always reflected a more transient society and a more accelerated life rhythm. Buildings in large cities, for example, are put up and pulled down seemingly overnight. Members of a lower economic bracket in America can raise themselves by hard work far more easily and quickly than their counterparts in Europe, where class lines are more tightly drawn. The result is a shifting landscape and a shifting population unlike that of the rest of the Western world, encouraging still further change and, sometimes, rootlessness.

Wilder was influenced not only by this environment but by his reading of the French philosopher Henri Bergson, whose theory of time, utilized by many late nineteenth century writers, offered an intellectual challenge to the once-accepted stability of the universe. According to this concept, there is in reality no past, present, or future, since all are one. For instance, suppose you ask the time of a passerby at a particular moment; in the interval it takes him to look at his watch—which registers, say, 2:15 P.M.—and give you an answer, a second has already passed. Another example: an out-of-town friend is staying at a hotel in your city for perhaps a week. You make an appointment to call on that friend at a certain hour. When you knock at the door, you know that behind it you will find a familiar face. Eight days later, if you were to knock at that same hotel-room door, a stranger would open it. And all because time has passed. This new assessment of time, added to Wilder's experiences as a student of archaeology (someone in the world of "now" digging up the remnants of a civilization of "then"), exerted an enormous influence on his thinking.

Finally, Wilder's peripatetic childhood and its exposure to many different, exotic cultures made space inconsequential, for it became easier, thanks to twentieth-century travel, to move from place to place, and easiest of all to let the imagination become the real scene-shifter. "The Long Christmas Dinner" asks the audience to recognize that "ninety years are to be traversed in this play, which represents in accelerated motion ninety Christmas dinners in the Bayard household."

As in *Our Town,* the play is concerned with the daily routine of average people. The major preoccupations are with birth, marriage, sickness, old age, and death. Wilder fixes the play in "real" time, as the title suggests, by choosing Christmas as the focal point: it is an occasion that unites most families, it has the feeling of a ritual (tradition), and, of course, it does have (or should) a religious significance. The family in this play gathers around the table, representing the present; at one end of the stage is a door, indicating birth, at the other end a portal, indicating death. The process of aging is shown very simply by the use of wigs and shawls. And, as in *Our Town,* the properties are kept to a minimum: the characters pantomime eating and in every way supply an imaginative, unrealistic counterpoint to the real events of the story.

There is, in fact, no story. Mother Bayard, sitting at the table with her family, remembers the Indians who were part of the early American experience. After a while she says she feels tired, rises, and walks out—toward the portal of death. Cousin Brandon puts on a white wig; a perambulator is wheeled on stage from the opposite portal—life ebbs and flows. The son Roderick gets up and moves toward the portal of death, then returns, for, as we can imagine, his illness has not proved fatal. Finally he, too, must go—but he makes his exit with astonishment, as if he can't grasp why. Another baby is wheeled across the stage toward the portal of death: it never had the chance to grow up and take its place at the table. And another generation now sits in the parental place, some of them using the very phrases their mothers and fathers had used when they were young. A middle-aged man reflects that the war is not a bad thing, since it releases the poisons that collect in nations; but *his* son is drafted, and rises and walks toward the portal of death, tossing aside his white wig, for he did not grow old on his way to that final door. Another son disappears from the scene because he is a

rebel against his family and runs off to China. Finally
only old cousin Ermengarde is left, and as she moves
toward the door the play ends.

A good deal of the dialogue consists of repetition,
another device that Wilder was to make use of in future
plays, particularly after Gertrude Stein had explained
her belief in its effectiveness as a means of underscoring
the cycle of life. The repetition at times verges on
monotony: after listening to a Christmas sermon one of
the Bayard wives remarks, "Lovely, I cried and cried."
The next generation is to say exactly the same thing.
Since almost a century passes in the course of this play
and yet nothing actually "happens," we are confronted
by the dramatic contrast between eternity and finite-
ness. One effect is to make us feel as though we have
boarded a train that originated further back and that we
will leave when our time comes; but the train will go
hurtling on, disgorging future passengers and taking on
still others, but never stopping for long.

"The Happy Journey to Trenton and Camden"
makes use of the flow of time and also introduces a
Stage Manager, who will function importantly in *Our
Town* and *The Skin of Our Teeth*. We are told that "no
scenery is required in this play," while the Stage Manager, holding a script in front of him, tells us what the
minor characters have to say, very much in the manner
of his successor in *Our Town*. Again, nothing much
"happens." The Kirby family, lower middle class Americans, take a drive in a car that is really four chairs.
(Wilder returns to this device in his cycle of plays *The
Seven Ages of Man:* a father and his children in "Child-

hood" make just such a trip.) At the beginning the
children are occupied in the ordinary way: the boy,
Arthur, is playing marbles; his sister, Caroline, is chat-
tering with her friends. During the course of the trip
the family engages in purely trivial activities: they eat
hot dogs, admire the billboards, stop at a gas station,
admire the scenery. And the language they speak is
unpretentious, unadorned, even unintellectual. But we
are not allowed to believe in their "reality" for long,
since the Stage Manager interrupts from time to time
and reminds us that they are only actors performing a
role. It is this device of placing them at a distance that
keeps them from sounding sentimental or uninteresting.

Bertolt Brecht, a German playwright who began his
career in Berlin in the 1920's, had developed a concept
of theater that insisted emotional moments should be
interrupted by constant reminders to the audience that
they were watching only an illusion of life: there was to
be no attempt at copying "reality." He called this idea
Verfremdung, or "Alienation," and its purpose was to
instruct the public rather than to encourage it to wallow
in sentiment. But long before Brecht popularized this
theory, Wilder was experimenting along similar lines.
In this respect he was not an innovator, of course; nor
was Brecht entirely. Both had been strongly influenced
by the Expressionistic movement that grew up in Germany after World War I (there the goal was a didactic
theater in which the theme or "message" was more
important than the characters, who were drawn as
abstracts, while the tightly knit plot was discarded in

favor of episodic scenes). Wilder had enough of a sense of the future to realize that some new treatment of ideas had to be employed in the theater if it was not to die of sameness and stodginess. Possibly the most important aspect of the Kirbys' "happy journey" is the reason for it, which we do not really discover until the end. Mrs. Kirby wants to visit her married daughter, but this is no ordinary visit: she comes to comfort the young woman because her baby has died at birth: "God thought best, dear. God thought best. We don't understand why. We just go on, honey, doin' our business." So argued Captain Alvarez, trying to give solace to Estaban, grieving for his dead twin brother; so believed the pre-Christian Captain Philocles in *The Woman of Andros.* Basically, Wilder's philosophy remained unchanged; what altered was his perception of how to display it.

The most original and ambitious play in the volume is "Pullman Car Hiawatha." Again a Stage Manager is present, but this time Wilder searches for universal types rather than particular members of a family. Consequently there is only one couple on the train— Philip and Harriet; the other passengers are a Maiden Lady, a Doctor, A Woman of Fifty, Two Engineers, a Porter, and an Insane Woman. The train, naturally, is a symbol not only of movement in space but of passage of time as it roars to its destination, and of course it is one of Wilder's favorite devices for indicating rootlessness. As in *Our Town,* the Stage Manager tells us about the car on its way to Chicago: he is very definite about the time, which is December 21, 1930. He invites the audience to listen to the other characters as they think;

then actors enter, representing towns, fields, villages (including Grover's Corners of future fame). Others representing tramps, mechanics, passengers, come by, describing places in America and events that have occurred. Finally Time itself makes its appearance: the Minutes are gossips, the Hours are philosophers, the Years theologians. The Planets join them, speaking no words, only uttering vague sounds. At the end the archangels Michael and Gabriel board the train: they have come to fetch Harriet, who is dying. At first she refuses to accompany them; then she bids good-bye to the town, the shops, the wallpaper (this is certainly Emily of *Our Town*), and slips away. As the play closes, the train, now in the Chicago depot, is boarded by attendants who begin to clean the cars. And so the cycle of life—and death—goes.

To dramatize further the concept of the circle of life, Wilder gives to the Hours dialogue taken from the great philosophers. Spinoza's words are quoted by one, observing that the "common occurrences of daily life are vain and futile." Plato is quoted by another, "How will a man choose the ruler that shall rule over him: Will he not choose a man who has first established order in himself . . . ?" The quote from Aristotle notes that quality called divine which man possesses sometimes but God has always. And the passage concludes with the quote from Genesis concerning the creation of Heaven and Earth and the command "Let there be light." Greek and Jew, classical source and Biblical, pre-Christian and post-Christian world, all blend and harmonize. But only when there is a sense of order. Therefore, although the death of Harriet is sad, that too is part of the natural order. It is even sadder that the Insane Woman, who has moments of lucidity that would shame a sane person, wishes to go with Gabriel and Michael in Harriet's place; but she cannot, for it is not her time but Harriet's that has come. And that is a further sign that the pattern exists, even though it is incomprehensible to us.

"The Happy Journey" will be developed more fully in *Our Town,* when, in effect, the Kirby family of the shorter play is studied in depth. And "Pullman Car Hiawatha" will blossom into *The Skin of Our Teeth,* with its use of philosophy, theology, literature, history, and the entire panorama of the cosmos. Although the earlier plays have both charm and interest, they are in a way blueprints for Wilder's two major theater pieces. Meanwhile, the simplicity and "realism" of the dialogue in *The Long Christmas Dinner* was carried over into his next work: his translation of *Lucrèce,* from the French of André Obey, attempted a language that was modern and unadorned. Wilder was a great admirer of Obey, who was not only a playwright but an actor and the manager of a troupe in Paris called the Compagnie de Quinze. And there was much in Obey's style that attracted Wilder's interest: like a number of outstanding French dramatists, Obey found nothing "escapist" in using material based on the classics. Obey was also to deal with Biblical themes in his play *Noé,* in which he concerns himself with the story of the Flood, the Ark, and Divine Justice. Indirectly, his character of Noah was to serve as a model for Mr. Antrobus in *The Skin of Our Teeth.*

Since Wilder had shown such an affinity for the

themes of antiquity, it is probable that the story of the rape of Lucrèce suggested to audiences another occasion for more of his beautiful prose. They seemed disconcerted by the translation's simplicity (Wilder had obviously abandoned his study of Cardinal Newman for his exploration of Jonathan Swift, whose sarcastic personality must have been in many ways antipathetic to him). Despite an outstanding cast headed by Katharine Cornell as Lucrèce, Brian Aherne as Tarquin, Blanche Yurka as First Narrator, and Brenda Forbes as Marina; despite sets and costumes by Robert Edmond Jones, music by Deems Taylor, and direction by Guthrie McClintic, the play, which opened at the Belasco Theatre on December 20, 1932, was not successful. For the next three years Wilder occupied himself working on another novel and learning more and more, as he put it, from the teachings of Gertrude Stein. For one of Wilder's most attractive qualities is that while he is perfectly capable of dropping into the lecturer's manner when he is talking to others (no doubt a carry-over from his former teaching days), his avidity for fresh ideas and new horizons makes him a perpetual student in the best sense. And Miss Stein, who dearly loved the role of mentor, must have been enchanted by his deference and admiration. At a party, when Picasso read his own verse, Wilder obligingly translated from Spanish into French for Miss Stein. They visited each other constantly; they even spoke of writing a book together: she was to supply the plot, he the words. (In the end she wrote the book, *Ida,* herself.) They exchanged long letters when they were apart; he wrote introductions to her books. And from this exposure to her ideas Wilder was able to sort out his own.

In some ways her point of view merely coincided with, or confirmed, his. Her concept of religion was very similar to Wilder's. As he was later to point out, "Religion, as Miss Stein uses the term, has very little to do with cults and dogmas, particularly in America . . . . Religion is what a person knows—knows beyond knowing, knows beyond anyone's power to teach him." In *Our Town* the Stage Manager expresses his convictions about the poets (and the saints) who understand instinctively the miracle of living. Again, it is obvious that in writing *The Long Christmas Dinner* Wilder was not deeply interested in character in a psychological sense: he was far more interested in what the character represented symbolically. Whereas the realistic playwright tried to draw a recognizable, particular portrait and from that point give it universal application, Wilder tried the reverse: he began with the universal and from it derived the particular. This technique was Brecht's also, but it would be equally fair to say that the unknown author of the fifteenth-century play *Everyman* probably had the same aim in mind. Therefore Gertrude Stein's insistence that characters have more life and effectiveness when they are imagined (she cites Vasari and Plutarch, who brought vividness to the biographies they wrote simply by stating the facts and letting the reader's fancy provide the rest), struck a responsive chord in Wilder, who had reached the same conclusion himself.

But in two areas she did contribute a great deal to his

work. After the critical hostility accorded *The Woman of Andros,* Wilder was clearly concerned about finding a subject that would please him without sounding as though it were escapist. His rediscovery of America coincided with Miss Stein's *Geographical History of America,* a shrewd appraisal of its weaknesses and strengths. In a letter he told her his opinion of her book, for which he was to write the introduction:

> What a book! I mean what a book! I've been living for a month with ever-increasing intensity on the conceptions of Human Nature and the Human Mind, and on the relations of Masterpieces to their apparent subject matter. Those things . . . have become cell and marrow in me . . . . Yes, I'm crazy about America. And you did that to me, too.

While Wilder was liberating himself from the elegances of Walter Pater and George Moore—two British writers known for their rarified style—and abandoning the hothouse prose of *The Woman of Andros* in favor of a simpler expression, as demonstrated by *The Long Christmas Dinner,* Gertrude Stein reminded him that "melody should be a by-product it should never be an end in itself . . . ." What she was advocating, of course, was an end to imitation and to consciously "pretty" writing, and a blending of form with content. He left off copying writers of another age and another country because he realized that the European sense of space, time, and identity were unlike the American: "Those senses are not ours and the American people and American writers have long been engaged in reshaping the inherited language to express modes of apprehension." Gertrude Stein's observation that it is "something strictly American to conceive a space that is filled with moving" reinforced Wilder's discovery. He could admit, finally, that "elevation and intensity are not solely and inseparably associated with noble images . . . . The United States is a middle class nation and has widened and broadened and deepened the concepts of the wide and the broad and the deep without diminishing the concept of the high." Gertrude Stein wanted language to do something and so stay alive; Wilder, following her lead, renounced the influence of older British writers, seeing in the new freedom and the search for a diction that would express the present the quality that made America unique: the openness of its society.

Every young writer is engaged in the struggle to throw off past styles: Somerset Maugham has recounted his infatuation with the prose of Oscar Wilde, which drove him to the British Museum, where he researched the names of rare gems and catalogued them in his notebook, waiting for a story he could invent that would have need of such exotic jewels. Happily he, too, discovered Swift and the beauty of lean prose in time and began to strip down his style as ruthlessly as Wilder. The latter was a little slower in arriving at the same goal post; in the end he might have come to it alone. As it happened, Gertrude Stein encouraged, if she did not initiate, his quiet revolution. Thanks to her, he learned how to look at his native land and draw inspiration from it for his books; thanks to her, he learned how to recast his philosophical concepts in a more appealing manner;

thanks to her, he learned the grace of simplicity and economy. The result of this process of "education" was that Wilder produced two of his most distinguished works in this period: a novel and a play.

Heaven's My Destination, written in 1935 but set in the American Midwest of 1930, derived its title, Wilder tells us, from a doggerel verse of the day; children wrote it in their schoolbooks, filling in the blank places:

> ———is my name;
>   America's my nation;
> ———is my dwelling place
>   And Heaven's my destination.

For the epigraph of the novel Wilder uses a statement made by Chrysis in *The Woman of Andros:* "Of all the forms of genius, goodness has the longest awkward age." For Wilder believes that living is itself an art and that, like art, it requires a kind of genius.

As with almost all of Wilder's novels, the structure is episodic: it begins with a journey (on a train, as usual) and ends with the hero traveling on; we leave him before he has reached his destination. In the course of the trip, which is spiritual as well as actual, he encounters different people and undergoes various experiences in the best tradition of picaresque fiction. This type of fiction enjoyed tremendous popularity all over Europe in the eighteenth and nineteenth centuries, for it allowed the novelist to describe any number of exciting adventures and at the same time introduce the reader to sections of the country and landscapes with which he might not be familiar, much as a camera might do. It was an ideal choice for Wilder's particular purpose, since it enabled him to combine a picture of Midwestern America with a young man's religious pilgrimage. Although Samuele in *The Cabala* is introduced to the reader as a traveler to Rome, once he arrives there the atmosphere of the book becomes hermetically sealed by the lives of the people who have banded together and retreated to the past. But *Heaven's My Destination* is open-ended, and, in contrast to the earlier novel, its pace is rapid, its style free, its tone comic. The comedy is achieved through the confrontation between irreconcilables: a young man tries to impose order on life, but life stubbornly refuses to be arranged so neatly. He arrives preaching the Gospel of nonviolence as taught and lived by the Indian statesman Mahatma Gandhi; his hearers are more interested in the Message of Mammon. His interpretations of the Bible are literally correct and entirely logical; but the essence of human nature is its illogic. And so he reels from error to error, almost destroying himself in the struggle. In an article written in 1952 Wilder was to explain why George Brush's concept of the universe was so typically American: "Americans constantly feel that the whole world's thinking has to be done over again . . . . Americans start from scratch . . . every American . . . feels himself capable of being the founder of his own religion." If the novel does not contain too many references to the time in which it was written, it nevertheless captures one aspect of the American character.

Unlike Wilder's earlier novels, *Heaven's My Destination* is absolutely objective: no narrator intrudes, however briefly, to explain the situation or give the reader information not otherwise obtainable. The book is divided into thirteen chapters. Part I ends when a crisis threatens to impede the story—almost like a physical obstruction preventing the train from moving forward. When this crisis is resolved, Part II begins and the hero travels on. The end is again distinguished by a crisis, this time an almost fatal one; once more it is resolved, and the last the reader sees of George Brush he is happily riding into the future.

The events take place in the summer of 1930, immediately after the stock-market crash and the closing of the banks. From time to time mention is made of the economic disaster that has burst upon America, but it looms no larger than did the Napoleonic Wars in the books of Jane Austen, for Wilder is always concerned with the inner, moral pressures rather than the outer, physical ones. George is a textbook salesman, twenty-three years old, and a passionate believer in bettering himself and reforming others. In the course of his travels through Oklahoma City, Camp Morgan, Kansas City, and Ozarkville, Missouri, he becomes acquainted with people who have deep spiritual problems—or so he thinks, even if they do not—and he attempts to help them. In every case he either diagnoses incorrectly or offers the wrong remedy. At the same time, his own difficulties, of which he is genuinely unaware, are so numerous that he becomes a further source of comedy since he is unable to help himself.

One of the funniest scenes in the novel occurs when he is solemnly and sincerely describing his conversion to religion. As he tells it, when he was in college a sixteen-year-old girl led him to the truth. When he describes her and her activities, however, it is clear that she is a drug-addict, although George apparently has no inkling of the fact. He tells his acquaintances about another girl he was very fond of but had to renounce because she smoked; George looks on smoking as a mortal sin. He doesn't approve of banks, finding something immoral in their investments and usury. So suspicious is he of them that he draws out all his money, since he thinks it wrong for the money just to be lying there, piling up interest. At one point he describes a bank as shaky—meaning immoral—but his nervous listener, interpreting this as a comment on the bank's economic situation, alerts all his friends to the news that the bank is failing. And so everyone rushes to the bank to withdraw his savings, thus creating a panic and a run on a bank that was originally sound. George rides innocently away, never realizing what he has done.

He has other peculiar notions. He disapproves of salary raises when the country is in the midst of a depression. He refuses to travel on Sunday. He can explain every detail of his expense account, down to the last penny; not for him is the padded itinerary or hotel bill. Although he has an excellent singing voice, he won't accept money when he sings; he feels he has been blessed with a "gift" and so should not take financial advantage of it. Even his reason for the journey has a moral purpose: he reveals that he has "ruined" a girl and is determined to locate her and make an honest woman of her. The trouble is, he can't find the place where she lived. Altogether, George is an outrageous exaggeration of all the do-gooders in American fiction; but he is drawn with so much kindness and restraint that he never sounds like a caricature. And in his determination to give his money away and live with the same simplicity as Gandhi, he is, in fact, rather touching. His high-minded goals, juxtaposed with what he describes as his three greatest disappointments, again reduce the reader to helpless laughter: the tragedies of his life, thus far, are: (1) that he was not elected to a fraternity he wished to belong to in college; (2) that his religious teacher told him he had a closed mind and would never amount to anything; and (3) that he can't find the girl he "ruined."

Minor worries plague him: his literature teacher has suggested that *King Lear* was the greatest play ever written, but George, having read it several times, can't find anything in it. His solution: he memorizes it in its entirety, desperately believing that after he has absorbed the book physically, so to speak, he will achieve instant enlightenment. His greatest shock comes when a girl he considers "nice" tells him she believes in Darwin. Although Wilder uses the moral currency of the day—smoking, Darwinism, etc., as a means of dramatizing George's sense of outrage—these are merely convenient symbols; in another age a young man might be shocked by something else—the discovery, say, that his parents drink to excess. George is funny (and pathetic) not because he thinks *smoking* is wicked, but because he does not really understand what wickedness is.

Halfway through his journey he stops at Queenie's

boardinghouse, where the other roomers tolerate him because of his magnificent singing voice. Driven to despair by his excessive Puritanism, Herb and Morrie, two newspaper men; Bat, a mechanic in sound pictures; and Louie, once a hospital chemist but now an orderly because of the depression, talk him into believing he is "sick" and prescribe some medicine for him—which turns out to be alcohol. He becomes joyously drunk and wakes up the next morning happy that he has been cured of his mysterious ailment. As a final lesson they invite him to a Sunday dinner with some friends; the house is really a bordello, but George never learns the truth. He thinks the young ladies are absolutely charming (possibly his good opinion of them moves them to their best behavior), and so disgusts his four friends because of his stupidity that in a rage they beat him up. They have tried to corrupt him with drink and women—and he remains hopelessly incorruptible. But he is deeply wounded by their cruelty and decides the only explanation is that they are all crazy.

Taking to the road once more, he encounters fraudulence again. James Bigelow is a professional salvationist, but when he realizes that George actually *believes* in the Bible, Bigelow beats a hasty retreat: he is unnerved by the sight of someone who actually tries to practice what he, Bigelow, preaches, like a nightmare turning real. A woman George meets professes to be a spiritualist, and toward her George is very unforgiving, for he feels she takes money from ignorant people while playing on their wish to communicate with their dead. When he sees a boy insulting an old schoolteacher, he knocks the boy down, then reproaches himself for not behaving more like Gandhi. When he finally locates the girl he has been searching for, she refuses his offer of marriage; to his horror, she doesn't feel a bit "ruined." In this world, people simply don't act the way George expects them to, and the discovery is very unsettling. George has a formula for right action, but no one is interested in the brew.

The second major crisis of his life occurs when he offers to look after the child of Herb, who is dying; although Herb was deeply involved in tormenting George before, he learns that George is the only one who cares about the little girl. Going into a shop to buy a doll for her, George sees another little girl in the store. Because she has behaved badly her parents are punishing her, but when George tries to cheer her up he is accused of being a child molester. (The little girl happily supports this accusation as a wonderful way to make her parents feel sorry for her and so forgive her: young though she is, she is more corrupt than George.) Meanwhile, the premises have been entered by a holdup man (who is so inept that he might have belonged to The Lavender Hill Mob or the gang in the film *Rififi:* his major trouble is that the handkerchief which he has tied across his face keeps slipping down). Since the shopkeeper in a burst of confidence had told George she no longer keeps money in the cash-register but secretes it on a shelf, as a means of thwarting thieves, George, in a passion to reform the burglar, tells him where the real hidingplace is. Naturally, he not only enrages the woman who owns the shop but annoys the burglar, too, for the burglar doesn't want to be uplifted in this way. And equally naturally, George is arrested on two charges: aiding and abetting a criminal and "kidnapping" a child.

In prison he shares a cell with another George, last name Birkin (George's other ego?), who has been arrested as a Peeping Tom. Birkin defends himself by saying that when he looks into windows he sees people as they really are, not as they pretend to be in company, and that is why he cannot be tolerated: the world does not like others to know the truth about itself. By this time the judge learns that George Brush has already been arrested twice before: once because he rode in a "Jim Crow" car (when asked why, he simply noted that he believed in equality of race) and once because he was held responsible for spreading false rumors concerning a bank's collapse. The court does not quite know what to make of this "character" who displays enthusiasm even when his picture is taken by the police photographer and inquires if he can buy a few copies for himself. After George explains his philosophy to the judge, his belief in "ahimsa" (giving people a chance to better their lives, as he understands its meaning), and his admiration for the Russian novelist Leo Tolstoi, he is released. The judge, a kindly man, respects George but thinks him very peculiar for trying to apply such simple solutions to such complex questions. It is a funny sight to see George leaving the town, already established in legend as the terror of the territory.

In his genuine goodness, George successfully bails out George Birkin, his cellmate. Although Birkin likes

George and is grateful to him, they part in anger after a drive along the road, when Birkin jeers at George for his religious convictions. Birkin is the voice of reason challenging intuitive faith. And of course, as Wilder demonstrates, the two must always remain enemies, for in the end faith cannot be "proven": it simply "is." George is further shaken in his beliefs when he meets Lottie, the sister of the girl he still wants to marry, and she tells him that Roberta had been pregnant with his child, which she aborted. Loaded down by a guilt too great for him to bear alone, George finally prevails on Roberta to marry him, though there is now no need. Nor does he love her. It is simply his moral duty. She consents more out of indifference than anything else, and they adopt Herb's daughter, Elizabeth. But the marriage is not a success. George disintegrates rapidly, but being George he achieves that in a unique way, too: he takes up smoking, learns German, earns a lot of money, loses his faith—and falls ill.

His physical sickness is a sign of his spiritual bankruptcy, and his darkest moment comes when, in the hospital, he tells the chaplain that religion is a fraud. At the end of his rope, George contemplates suicide. But before he can take action, a silver spoon is sent to him by a Catholic priest, Father Pasziewski, who is dying. The priest had never met George but had heard much about his goodness from Queenie's boarders; along with the spoon go the priest's prayers for George. The moment is all the more mysterious since the two do not know each other. But their shadows have touched. Looking at the spoon, George no longer feels lonely. At the end, we watch him boarding the train, once more embarking on his heavenly mission.

The book is remarkable in many ways. George Brush is the most vivid character Wilder had yet created, the dialogue the best he had yet written. If depression America was not reflected in the novel, at least the quality of American life, the curious blend of cynicism and naiveté that is so uniquely American in spirit, were here. The book is also remarkably objective in its view of the American ideal, yet sympathetic to the national weaknesses that blur the principles. All that is best and worst, wisest and silliest, kindest and cruelest, meanest and most generous in the story of this country is epitomized in George, who, on this occasion, isn't merely a symbol. He is a person.

George's failure lies in the fact that, first, he discovers the existence of sin (when his "friends" not only corrupt him but beat him up, for instance) not as a theory but as a condition of life; and second, that he cannot come to terms with it by compromise. (As has been noted before, the premise of Graham Greene's *The Quiet American* is exactly the same: the "hero" of the British novel might well be George in Vietnam thirty years later.) Taken in a larger sense, this ingenuousness characterized Woodrow Wilson's relations with the Big Four after World War I. Wilson had a vision (right or wrong) of a European community in which all would be equally represented, but by the time he came to the bargaining table at Versailles, the European powers had pretty well carved things up to their own liking; and Wilson's Fourteen Points were simply one of the persuasions used to cajole the Germans into surrender. The American enigma has always been that of a nation which in an incredibly short time so accelerated its history that in the space of one century it became a superpower, yet which almost always found itself politically on the short end of the stick. The same ruthlessness and charity that marks the development of the United States reflects itself in George Brush. He is almost hopeless. Yet the spoon that is willed to him holds out some possibility for future change—perhaps no more than we see in Samuel Beckett's world when a weak green shoot appears at the end of *Waiting for Godot,* the setting for which is as arid as a desert. But Wilder certainly believes that change is possible: it simply depends on the individual.

If George is perhaps a failure, Birkin is totally and unquestionably so. To Birkin, the world is bounded by the five senses, rational solutions, practical considerations, material concerns. Therefore, the magic and the mystery of existence will always be beyond him. We can, for example, explain the process whereby an acorn becomes an oak tree; science may someday be able to produce more impressive creations than nature. But though we know the "how" of it, does the botanical explanation give us the "why"? And when we have finished demonstrating that genius is sublimation or compensation or neurosis, do we really know why one madman is also a poet and the other merely a schizophrenic? Above all, can we *ever* know? Birkin, and science, would be inclined to say yes; Wilder, and George, would have to say no.

And so, despite his follies and imperfections, George

is not entirely laughable or easily dismissed. He has simply not yet reached his destination—for "goodness has the longest awkward age."

The novel confused a number of critics when it first appeared. Wilder himself noted that some thought it was the portrait of a saint, others believed it was a satire on a ridiculous fool. Still others suggested it was some kind of a joke and took Wilder to task for being frivolous at such a moment in America's history. Sigmund Freud, who had been overwhelmed with admiration for *The Bridge of San Luis Rey,* was revolted by *Heaven's My Destination;* he did not understand why Wilder wanted to write a book about an "American fanatic" and threw the book away in anger. But Gertrude Stein loved it. She was quite right.

Perhaps one reason why the book is so memorable, particularly when compared with the "angry" novels of those times, is that Wilder based his major character on a real person, or rather, on real people. He tells us that George Brush had about him a little of Gene Tunney (who also carried classics around and passionately loved literature); a little of Wilder's brother, Amos; a little of Wilder's father, who was a strict Calvinist, a letter-of-the-religious-law man; and a little of Wilder himself. He looked on the book as an effort to come to terms with his background (not only Calvinism, but the missionary schools in China and the religious atmosphere at Oberlin), and concluded, "The comic spirit is given to us in order that we may analyze, weigh and clarify things in us which nettle us, or which we are outgrowing or trying to reshape." While all the elements that had interested him in previous books are here—the classical tradition, humanism, intuitive faith, the meaning of life, the search for a pattern—they are leavened by a marvelous objectivity that recognizes the plight of the human condition; but in its moment of greatest anguish it recognizes also the absurdity—a technique Chekhov would have appreciated and admired. The earnestness is balanced by a humor not often found in Wilder.

Ultimately, the success he achieved with the character of George raises another question: whether Wilder might not have been wiser to concentrate more on the real and the particular rather than on the symbolic and the universal. But he had made his choice in the latter direction, and from that choice, three years later, in January of 1938, came *Our Town*.

A few years after *Our Town* was produced Wilder drew up some principles that, he believed, defined the drama. They serve so admirably as the backbone for all his plays that they make a useful introduction to them.

Wilder stressed, first of all, the fact that the theater was an art that demanded many collaborators and therefore needed intervening "executants"—that is, actors, directors, and designers upon whom the interpretation would depend. Thus he mentioned a production of *The Merchant of Venice* that was played with a maximum of sympathy for Shylock; yet Wilder himself recalled a performance he had seen in which the great French actor Fermin Gémier presented Shylock as a vengeful and hysterical buffoon, while Portia was a *gamine* from the Paris streets. Both points of view are equally interesting, both equally valid. Therefore, for Wilder,

> Characterization in a play is like a blank check which the dramatist accords to the actor for him to fill in—not entirely blank, for a number of indications of individuality are already there, but to a far less definite and absolute degree than in the novel . . . . The dramatist's principal interest being the movement of the story, he is willing to resign the more detailed aspects of characterization to the actor . . . .

Although his example of *The Merchant* does not really prove his case, for Shylock is not an abstract but a very sharply drawn character, the argument tells us something about Wilder's notion of theatrical characterization. Just as he rejected the realism of the depression-oriented novel, he rejected the realism of detailed portraiture such as O'Neill was giving the American theater in plays like *Desire Under the Elms.* Brecht had reduced his characters to deliberate symbols in order to enhance the political beliefs he held; Wilder used the same means to clarify his religious beliefs. In any theater that is essentially didactic the characters are obviously less important than the message.

Another theory that Wilder propounded was that the action in a play "takes place in a perpetual present time . . . . Novels are written in the past tense . . . . On the stage it is always now." In addition, the novel has the advantage of an omniscient author who can tell his readers facts that the other characters do not know; on a stage everything must be presented between the characters. Wilder pointed out that the Greek Chorus performed just such a function in the theater, and he believed that the modern playwright had to find an equivalent—as he was to do in supplying the Stage Manager for *Our Town*. A play thus provided with a Stage Narrator attains a kind of timelessness, for the narrator can be part of the play's momentary action and yet be a commentator on what has happened in the past; or he can look into the future and tell the audience what he sees, for he is both enclosed in finite time and stands beyond, outside it. Finally, if he can move back and forth in time so freely, he must be aware of the repetitions of history and the ideas that flow from one century to the next, and so he becomes a transmitter of myth, legend, allegory. In such a theater the characters are analogous not to the planets, which "wander," but to the stars, which are fixed; while the background or setting, like the earth itself, moves in time.

Observing that the theater is a world of pretense, Wilder ennumerated such conventions as the playing of women's roles by men in the Greek (and Elizabethan) age; the use of metric speech, although in life people do not speak verse; the reliance on masks and other devices. And he argued that these conventions did not spring from naiveté but from the vitality of the public imagination: they provoked the audience into participating instead of having all the work done for them by the dramatist. Even more important, in Wilder's estimation, the action was thereby raised from the specific to the general. In Shakespeare's world Juliet was not a "real" girl living in a "real" house cluttered with "real" furnishings; she was played by a boy on a bare stage and so became not a particular person but all the star-crossed heroines who have ever lived and who will live in the future. By Wilder's definition, theatrical pretense is absolutely essential to reinforce his theories of time.

Because drama is a collective experience, in Wilder's words, because it appeals to the "group-mind," it has about it the excitement of a festival, a coming together to celebrate an event. And so ritual must be part of drama in some fashion. It may be based on a typical evening during a particular season of the year, like "The Long Christmas Dinner." The details of the ritual are not important, but it must have enough familiarity about it to be recognizable as a convention to the audience. Equally, the material must be broad enough in scope to reach a large number of people *simultaneously,* and this need demands a subject-matter that is common to ordinary experience.

Our Town is, therefore, the blossoming of Wilder's theories. Emily and George are types rather than individuals, outlines rather than photographs. Although the play begins in America's past (between 1901 and 1913), it deals with the future, too. For in the end, Emily, having died, comes back to visit Grover's Corners; she exists simultaneously in all three pockets of time. The Stage Manager constantly reminds us of the make-believe quality of the play by asking us to imagine this or that prop; he himself plays different roles in addition to his own; he is not limited by sex, since he takes the part of Mrs. Morgan as well as of other men in the town; and from time to time he comments on the weather or the state of the world, lectures to the audience, and interprets the actions of the characters for us. Wilder even succeeds in supplying us with ritual: the hum of activity that makes up everyday life. One might almost say that brushing one's teeth or one's hair is a ritual; Wilder picks up moments like these to affirm that all of us are bound together in one vast chain, because we all share certain common thoughts and actions. There is a moment in James Joyce's *Portrait of the Artist* when Stephen thinks about God, who, he knows, is called "Dieu" in French, and God can always tell the nationality of the boy praying to Him by the language that is used. The mere idea of a French boy offering a simple prayer to "Dieu" (whose real name is God anyway, Stephen asserts), while at the same time an Irish boy is praying in *his* own language and so on across the universe, is enough to give Stephen a headache, for where does infinity end? But it is exactly this feeling that Wilder is after: we are all one in the One. As one of his characters in *Our Town* says:

> I never told you about that letter Jane Crofut got from her minister when she was sick. The minister of her church in the town she was in before she came here. He wrote Jane a letter and on the envelope the address was like this: It said: Jane Crofut, The Crofut Farm; Grover's Corners; Sutton County; New Hampshire; United States of America.

When the other character wants to know what is funny about that, the girl answers:

But listen, it's not finished: the United States of
America; Continent of North America; Western
Hemisphere; the Earth; the Solar System; the Universe; the Mind of God—that's what it said on the
envelope . . . . And the postman brought it just the
same.

And the other character comments, "What do you
know!"

Small-town America had already been discovered by
Edgar Lee Masters in *Spoon River Anthology* and Sinclair
Lewis in *Main Street,* to name only two examples. What
Wilder did was to take the same kind of subject and
relate it to both time and eternity. He chose New
England because of its deep roots in tradition; he chose
the period just before World War I so that he could
show that region as yet untouched by international
conflicts and barely brushed by industrialization.

When the play begins, there is no curtain and no
scenery. The audience, entering, sees an empty stage;
presently the Stage Manager, pipe in mouth, appears
and begins moving a table and some chairs around. He
waits patiently for the late arrivals in the theater, then
opens the play by announcing its title, author, producer,
director, and cast. He identifies the town in particular
detail: "just across the Massachusetts line: longitude 42
degrees 40 minutes; latitude 70 degrees 37 minutes . . . . The time is just before dawn . . . ." And a
cock crows. The Stage Manager then explains the layout
of the town and delivers a little gossip about some of its
citizens. Then the newspaper boy (an important symbol
in the play) delivers his papers; the town awakens to the
sound of breakfast preparations and getting children

off to school, and the cycle begins. Instead of lowering a curtain, Wilder chooses to telescope time by letting the Stage Manager announce to us that he is "skipping a few hours" in the day to show us some other scenes. He asks a professor of anthropology to step forward and explain the origin of the town's population; then the editor of the town paper explains the "political" situation, and so on. His comment on Grover's Corners is, "Very ordinary town, if you ask me. Little better behaved than most. Probably a lot duller." In truth, the most serious transgressor is the town drunk. Stimson.

The Stage Manager tells the audience that he is going to have a copy of the play put in the cornerstone of the new bank so that thousands of years from now people will know what life in Grover's Corners was like. He reflects: "Y'know—Babylon once had two million people in it, and all we know about 'em is the names of the kings and some copies of wheat contracts and . . . the sales of slaves. Yet, every night all those families sat down to supper, and the father came home from his work, and the smoke went up the chimney—same as here . . . ." And George's sister, Rebecca, sums up this sense of wonder in the first act: "George, is the moon shining on South America, Canada and half the whole world?"

When the Stage Manager returns for Act II, he informs us that three years have gone by. He reminds us of events that have occurred meanwhile: Joe's brother has taken over his newspaper route (in moving through time the Stage Manager informs us of Joe's brilliant career in college and his subsequent death in France

after the war broke out: "all that education for nothing"). Babies have been born, old people have died. And
a lot of young ones have fallen in love and married. He
sets the tone for this act also. Whereas "The First Act
was called the Daily Life . . . this Act is called Love and
Marriage." George and Emily suddenly become aware
of each other, poignantly, haltingly. But we never see
him propose. The Stage Manager introduces some
further accounts of the town, thus interrupting the
scene between the young people, and afterward he
simply informs us that we are going to see a wedding.
The act concludes with the ceremony (another ritual);
the couple descends into the auditorium and rushes up
the aisle joyously. In this instant the audience has been
transformed into members of a congregation. But the
Stage Manager breaks even this illusion by announcing
that the act is over and that there will be a ten-minute
intermission, returning us, in the manner of Brecht, to
the reality of the location—a playhouse.

Nine years have passed between the second and third
acts; there have been many changes. "Horses are getting
rarer . . . . Young folks . . . want to go to the moving
pictures all the time . . . . Everybody locks their house
doors now at night." Before long we learn that we are in
a cemetery, according to the dialogue. And we learn
that Emily has died in childbirth. Suddenly she appears
from among the umbrellas (for it is raining), wearing a
white dress, longing to come back to life. She talks to the
other dead around her and realizes suddenly "how in
the dark live persons are. From morning till night, that's
all they are—troubled." Emily decides to choose a happy

day and live it over again, but the Stage Manager
cautions her against it: "You not only live it; but you
watch yourself living it." (Here Wilder has described the
moment he narrated through Chrysis in *The Woman of
Andros*.) Emily's dead mother-in-law says that there is no
point in going back, that she should "think only of
what's ahead and be ready for what's ahead." But Emily
cannot forget her past and happy life: "How can I ever
forget that life? It's all I know. It's all I had." Even
though she is warned that she will not regain what she
expects, she has to find out for herself. And so she
chooses her twelfth birthday. As one part of her lives
over that occasion, the other part of her watches—and it
is unbearable: "I can't go on . . . . It goes so fast. We
don't have time to look at one another . . . . I didn't
realize. So all that was going on and we never
noticed . . . . Good-bye to clocks ticking . . . . And food
and coffee. And new-ironed dresses and hot
baths . . . . and sleeping and waking up. Oh, earth,
you're too wonderful for anybody to realize you." And
she asks wistfully, "Do any human beings ever realize
life while they live it?—every, every minute?" But of
course they do not, except perhaps, as the Stage Manager notes, the saints and poets. In short, the geniuses at
living.

The town drunk, also dead, speaks witheringly of the
stupidity and meaninglessness of life: "To move about
in a cloud of ignorance ; . . . to spend and waste time as
though you had a million years. To be always at the
mercy of one self-centered passion or another. Now you
know—that's the happy existence you wanted to go back

and see." But Emily's mother-in-law reproaches him: what he is saying isn't the *whole* truth. And slowly the dead fade away, Emily realizing at last that the living don't understand much. The Stage Manager, like a caretaker closing down the house, notes that it is getting late, and almost everyone is asleep in Grover's Corners as the stars do "their old, old criss-cross journeys in the sky." He winds up his watch, calls out the time: "Eleven o'clock in Grover's Corners" (which is the same time in the theater, too) as the play ends. He advises everyone to get a good rest and bids them all good-night.

The play, then, which has covered nine years in time, has begun at dawn and ended at night. The first act showed us the lives of the two main families in their separate existences; in the second they were brought together by the marriage of the children; and in the third they were separated again by Emily's death. But Emily has left a child—which is her "bridge," her immortality. The sense of atmosphere is so strong that one leaves the theater convinced that crickets can be heard chirping in the darkness. For what the author has done is to *make* us participate, to fuse us into a homogeneous body, for a few hours; we are as much sharers in the action on stage as if we were in a church alternating our prayers with the priest at the altar. *Our Town* succeeds as ritual and as celebration.

One of the most interesting aspects of the play is the manner in which it observes the classical unities, although at first superficial glance it seems to violate them. There is certainly no subplot (one might even argue that there is no plot); the entire action takes place in Grover's Corners, maintaining the unity of place; and even though years pass, the morning-to-evening structure of the three acts suggests a kind of unity of time. Once again Wilder proved how ingenious he could be in observing certain traditional patterns, yet adapting them to his needs in such a fashion as to seem innovative.

The banality of the dialogue, the lack of characterization in the speeches themselves (sometimes it is almost impossible to tell *who* is speaking by the words alone), all contribute to the feeling of something timeless and universal. And the episodes, which are not really sequential, are introduced in such a way as to convey the flavor of life in its haphazard, zigzag motion. Finally, although the style of Tennessee Williams' *The Glass Menagerie* is very different, *Our Town* is, like the later drama, also a "memory" play; it re-creates a small American town as it once may have been and always will be in our remembrance. And its inhabitants are as frozen in time as the figures in John Keats's *Ode on a Grecian Urn*. Bearing in mind Gertrude Stein's belief that "beginning and ending is not really exciting. Moving is in every direction," Wilder added his own estimate of the play:

> It is an attempt to find a value above all price for the smallest events of our daily life. I have made the claim as preposterous as possible, for I have set the village against the largest dimensions of time and place. The recurrent words in this play (few have noticed it) are "hundreds," "thousands," and "mil-

lions." Emily's joys and griefs, her algebra lessons and her birthday presents—what are they when we consider all the billions of girls who have lived, who are living, and who will live?

That Wilder nevertheless believed in the individual experience is seen by a speech delivered to the Joyce Society in 1954:

> Though I realize that my joy or my grief is but "one" in the ocean of human life, nevertheless it has its reality. I know that the existential thing pouring up in me, my joy or my fear, is a real thing and yet that the intensity with which I feel it can be called absurd. It is absurd to claim that "I," in the vast reaches of time and place and repetition, is worth an assertion.

And he concluded that writers had to find new ways to understand the smallness of man in the vastness of the universe and yet show "the validity of the individual as an absolute."

What saves the play from cloying sentimentality is its sense of distance. Almost as the surrealists were to draw a portrait with three eyes, indicating that the frontal view and the profile were to be considered simultaneously, the audience, like Emily, zeros in on the action with a hand-held camera only to shift to a long-distance lens under the direction of the Stage Manager. It is therefore unnecessary to show conflict, sickness, pain, a deathbed scene. And this omission also contributes to the still-life quality of the play. It is obviously not a technique that would work with many subjects or ideas:

it is, in fact, limited in its possible application. But it represents an admirable blend of style and content; one cannot be separated from the other.

When the play was adapted to film, its producer, Sol Lesser, missed a good deal of what Wilder had intended. For example, Lesser had wanted to depict the wedding "realistically," without interruptions. Wilder fought the triteness of the concept, noting that at a ceremony the bride and the groom are thinking their separate thoughts; the guests are either admiring the couple or remembering their own wedding, and so on. By eliminating Wilder's devices, Lesser would have treated the moment conventionally and so diminished the idea—a great danger for such a generalized story, as Wilder warned him. He also worried about Lesser's filming of the Death-and-Immortality scene; as the speeches were rewritten, Wilder noted, they read "like a sweetness-and-light Aimee MacPherson spiel." And finally, Wilder cautioned that the changes made in Emily might turn her into something quite different from what he had intended. He did not want her to be pure-village-girl-sweet-ingenue: push the speeches "a few inches further and she becomes priggish."

The smallest shift in tone disturbed Wilder. Commenting on some added scenes in the film in which a child sneaked an extra doughnut, someone else took four spoonfuls of sugar in the coffee, a mother checked her son's state of cleanliness by looking behind his ears, Wilder wrote to Lesser: "A few more [such scenes] . . . and the audience would be justified in believing they are in one of those pictures Quaint Hayseed

Family Life." Wilder's attempts to avoid the pretty, the folksy, the cute, the tearful, are nowhere more apparent than in this exchange of correspondence, which suggests the careful balancing act of an angel on the head of a pin. He yielded finally to one alteration when Lesser worried about Emily's death as being too cruel and requested "a happy ending." Tactfully Wilder answered: "Insofar as the play is a generalized allegory, she dies—we die—they die; insofar as it is a concrete happening it's not important that she die . . . . Let her live—the idea will have been imparted anyway."

The play was, for the most part, a critical as well as a popular success. If Robert Benchley found it pretentious and unintelligent, the critic Mary McCarthy (in whose book Wilder ranked very low after *The Woman of Andros*) admired it, somewhat to her astonishment, and wondered whether something had happened to her standards! It enjoyed an enormous vogue abroad, particularly in the German-speaking countries: the Swiss playwright Friedrich Dürrenmatt, who later paid Wilder the compliment of acknowledging the influence of *Our Town* on his very different, much more theatrical tragicomedy *The Visit,* felt that Wilder had rendered locale "immaterial and transparent" and had contributed as much toward freeing the theater for the imagination as had Luigi Pirandello, the twentieth-century Italian dramatist and short-story writer.

Certainly in *Our Town* and in his other plays Wilder showed a link with Pirandello. The latter had attempted to liberate the conventional stage from its physical limitations by centering much of the action in the minds of the characters and by juggling such opposites as madness and sanity, falsehood and truth, illusion and reality, always asking which was which. Pirandello's is a theater where nothing is absolute or fixed, where everything is relative and fluid; and even when he sets his plays in a parlor his imagination lifts the spectator far beyond the room itself. This latter aspect of his work, its open-ended quality, most suggests what Wilder was trying to do. Added to the didacticism of Brecht and the freedom of Pirandello is another element in *Our Town,* the idea behind William Blake's quatrain:

> To see a World in a Grain of Sand
> And a Heaven in a Wild Flower,
> Hold Infinity in the palm of your hand
> And eternity in an hour.

Just as Wilder had surprised everyone by his shift in style when he wrote his novels (it was a long way from *The Woman of Andros* to *Heaven's My Destination*), he took them unawares again when, in December of the same year, 1938, he offered the public a new style of play for him, *The Merchant of Yonkers.* Although it was not successful until it was revised and restaged sixteen years later as *The Matchmaker,* it belongs essentially to this "discovery of America" phase of Wilder's career.

Written originally for Max Reinhardt to direct, in its second version it became the ideal vehicle for Ruth Gordon, particularly when Tyrone Guthrie was at the helm. The most frivolous of all Wilder's theater pieces, it still manages to capture both in style and content some of his favorite devices and theories.

For a long while Wilder had been in rebellion against "well made" plays with their tidy plots, carefully built climaxes, conveniently arranged situations, and puppetlike characters. They were popularized by two nineteenth-century French writers, Eugène Scribe and Victorien Sardou, and slavishly imitated well into the twentieth century. (Even Ibsen, disgusted with these mechanically written formulas that had nothing relevant to say about their times, was not averse to using one element—a methodically constructed story.) It occurred to Wilder that "one way to shake off the nonsense of the nineteenth century is to make fun of it." Accordingly, he made use of all the conventional ingredients of these plays, which took themselves very seriously. Wilder, however, turned them into farce.

The "hero" of *The Matchmaker* is a virtuous man by worldly standards, but by spiritual ones he is a miser. (The tone reflects Wilder's own struggles with the narrow Calvinism of his background.) Drawing on Molière for the character of the miser, as well as on Nestroy for the basic plot, Wilder manages to show the wonder and the joy in life that Horace Vandergelder cannot appreciate since he has spent all his days saving money and working. He has been as much a miser in his relationships with people as in his business affairs. It is only proper that he should get his just deserts and be punished in proportion to his crime. And he is, for he marries a woman who is determined to teach him what happiness is by squandering all his money.

Horace Vandergelder is sixty, self-righteous, self-satisfied. He also supplies whatever "villainy" exists in the play, for in a parody of Victorian melodrama Wilder makes him the one obstruction to his niece's happiness. Vandergelder disapproves of the young man Ermengarde is in love with: he follows the lowest of occupations in Vandergelder's estimation, for he is an artist. But Ambrose is quite as clever as Vandergelder and quite as unscrupulous about getting what he wants. Most of the plot is taken up with the young lovers' efforts to cajole or trick Vandergelder into giving consent to their marriage.

He is equally harsh with his employees. His clerk, Cornelius, always searching for some kind of adventure, feeling the need to live, is a source of exasperation to Vandergelder, whose mind is completely closed. In the end Cornelius has his adventure and marries a pretty little milliner, Irene Molloy, whom Vandergelder was contemplating for his own wife. At one blow Cornelius triumphs over his employer and follows his heart.

The characters are stock figures—designedly so. In a farce they cannot have much life anyway, for the audience is more interested in the fun on stage than in the people. At the same time, the form enabled Wilder to stand by his declaration that the theater was at its best in creating outlines or types rather than realistic characters. And so Cornelius typifies the young rebel (but his anger takes no more violent shape than blowing up his employer's tomato cans); Vandergelder is the villain (but his bark is worse than his bite); and Ermengarde and Ambrose are the devoted young lovers (but they are just a little stupid). The one glory of the play is the most realistically drawn character, Dolly Levi.

Dolly is Vandergelder's opposite in every way. He is

stingy; she is extravagant. He is closed in emotionally; she is outgoing, exuberant. He is preternaturally solemn; she sees laughter in everything. He shouts; she wheedles. He worries about the future; she cares only for the present. He regards himself as a cunning, ruthless man of the world; he is putty in her hands.

In the tradition of Victorian melodrama, Wilder gives the characters speeches that they deliver downstage, full-face, to the audience. This is, in part, Vandergelder's view of himself:

> Ninety-nine per cent of the people in the world are fools and the rest of us are in great danger of contagion. But I wasn't always free of foolishness as I am now. I was once young, which was foolish; I fell in love, which was foolish; and I got married, which was foolish; and for a while I was poor, which was more foolish than all the other things put together.

He goes on to tell the audience in confidence that after a while his wife died, which was foolish (in the earlier version of the play he calls it "sensible," thereby suggesting a meanness of character that the revision does not possess), and then he notes that he grew older, "which was sensible of me; then I became a rich man, which is as sensible as it is rare." He eventually confides that he is thinking of marrying again: "If I should lose my head a little, I still have enough money to buy it back. After many years' caution and hard work, I have a right to a little risk and adventure . . . ." He comes to Dolly, a matchmaker, to help him find a wife, little dreaming that she has picked herself out for the job.

Dolly has a philosophy, which she expresses. Early in

the play she tells about her dead husband, who was
Viennese, and adds: "I want New York to be more like
Vienna and less like a collection of tired and nervous
ants." And this husband of hers is still alive for her: she
speaks to him (and the audience) when she looks back
over her life:

> . . . Vandergelder's never tired of saying most of the
> people in the world are fools, and in a way he's right,
> isn't he? . . . But there comes a moment in every-
> body's life when he must decide whether he'll live
> among human beings or not—a fool among fools or
> a fool alone.

Wilder's Dolly—unlike his other characters—renounces
loneliness, but then this is a comedy. And she sums up:

> The surest way to keep us out of harm is to give us
> the four or five human pleasures that are our right
> in the world—and that takes a little *money!* . . .
> Money, a little *money!* . . . Money, . . . pardon my
> expression—is like manure; it's not worth a thing
> unless it's spread about encouraging young things to
> grow.

Francis Bacon had used the same analogy about money
more than three hundred years before, but it is still
funny and true.

As always with Wilder, the drama comes from the
collision of irreconcilables. But since Dolly is very
charming indeed, and very clever about getting what
she wants; and since Vandergelder is charming too,
reminding us of Walt Disney's Grumpy in *Snow White*

and the Seven Dwarfs rather than a real, moustache-twirling villain, the ending is bound to be cheerful. Everyone pairs off happily, and the younger clerk, Barnaby, sums it all up. When he is asked to explain what the play is about, he says:

> Oh, I think it's about . . . I think it's about adventure. The test of an adventure is that when you're in the middle of it, you say to yourself, "Oh, now I've got myself into an awful mess; I wish I were sitting quietly at home." And the sign that something's wrong with you is when you sit quietly at home wishing you were out having lots of adventures . . . .

One minor character, a new employee of Vandergelder, contributes, along with Dolly, to the Wilder philosophy:

> There are some people who say you shouldn't have any weaknesses at all—no vices. But if a man has no vices, he's in great danger of making vices out of his virtues, . . . No, no—nurse one vice in your bosom. Give it the attention it deserves and let your virtues spring up modestly around it . . . . Never support two weaknesses at the same time. It's your combination sinners—your lecherous liars and your miserly drunkards—who dishonor the vices and bring them into bad repute . . . .

Not only were the directorial touches better in the second version of the play; the writing was, too. Under Guthrie's guidance Dolly's soliloquy about money was much shorter and funnier; in *The Merchant of Yonkers* it had turned into a long lecture about "accepting life," sounding like a poor echo of *The Woman of Andros.* Vandergelder is drawn with greater sympathy the second time around: half the time when he does shabby things, like eavesdropping behind a screen, it is because other people suggest such measures; he does not adopt them on his own. The changes are slight, true; but they add up to the difference between charm and lack of it. Whenever a line in the earlier version threatened to become too sentimental, it was either toned down or cut altogether. Guthrie obviously kept a tight hand on the reins.

With its mistaken identities, people scurrying around the stage hiding in cupboards or slamming doors, screens collapsing or folding at the wrong moment, girls dressed as boys—with its boisterous activity *The Matchmaker* had all the ingredients necessary for its transformation into a musical—*Hello, Dolly!* Bustle and bounce were certainly not characteristic of Wilder's earlier plays; therefore, slight though *The Matchmaker* is, it is an interesting bridge between moods. Perhaps it merely reflected something he once said: "Our plays get happier as we get older."

As always, Wilder avoided anything that was contemporary in theme; he has never had much in common with the headlines of the moment. *Our Town* is pre–World War I in setting; *The Matchmaker,* earlier than that. Even the most consciously "modern" of his books, *Heaven's My Destination,* is moved back five years in time. The incredible shortsightedness of certain critics prevented them from realizing that the only way a situation can be appraised objectively is by some kind of distance, achieved either through a shift in time or place. (Someone named William Shakespeare seemed to approve of that theory, too.) Wilder had begun by using Italy, Greece, and South America to fill his canvas. The pressures of the American economic collapse and the forceful views of Gertrude Stein helped him to focus on material nearer home. But as always, it had to be studied at arm's length.

He had made two important discoveries. First, he saw that it was essential to be aware of the "totality" of the world picture; hence his assessment of Thoreau's retreat to Walden as parochial, and his admiration of Emily Dickinson, who "loved the particular while living in the universal." For Wilder, involvement, not retreat, was the only possible answer. And second, he recognized that it was exciting "being an American . . . converting necessity into volition." He decided that those who were most independent of spirit had left the Old World for the New. In a way, so had he.

5 THE WEAVING:
History Is *One* Tapestry

A year after Wilder finished *Our Town* Europe erupted into World War II; two years later America was also at war. As the cancer of Fascism spread, plunging once civilized and cultured nations into incredible acts of barbarism—the "wrong" people and the "wrong" books were burned indiscriminately—universal pessimism kept pace with it: the world seemed on the brink of a new Dark Age. Before he left America for service abroad, Wilder produced his answer to the holocaust: *The Skin of Our Teeth* (1942), a testament to his faith in the survival of Man. Its German title is perhaps even more apropos; it translates as *We've Come Through Once Again.*

Wilder himself has given us the best description of his play when contrasted with the earlier one: "*Our Town* is the life of a family seen from a telescope, five miles

away. *The Skin of Our Teeth* is the destiny of the whole
human group seen from a telescope 1,000 miles away."
The three acts treat of three different moments in the
creation of the world; the four major characters represent the types most prevalent in any society. And the
characters themselves in turn represent different levels
of meaning: they are actors, whose personal stories
filter through the lines they are reading; they are
Everyman and Everywoman; and they are the members
of a typical American family. The actual setting for Acts
I and III is the Antrobus home in Excelsior, New
Jersey; Act II takes place on the boardwalk in Atlantic
City. But as events continue to erupt, it is clear that the
actual location is anywhere and everywhere.

Act I begins as a lantern slide, projected on the
curtain, announces the name of the theater, and this is
followed by News Events of the World. It is interrupted
halfway through by a statement that a wedding ring has
been found by some cleaning-women in the theater
(three of them, like The Fates?) with the inscription "To
Eva from Adam. Genesis II:18." (The reference, of
course, is to God's promise to give Man a Helpmate.)
The news continues, concerning the excessive cold
reported in Vermont and Montreal, then shifting to a
picture of Mr. Antrobus' home. He is a celebrity who
"invented the wheel." He comes of very old stock "and
has made his way up from next to nothing. It is
reported that he was once a gardener" (Wilder's view of
Adam's occupation), but "left that situation under circumstances that have been variously reported." Another picture shows us Mrs. Antrobus holding her

roses: she was the inventor of the apron. And the play is off . . .

The maid, Sabina, begins by addressing the audience in a parody of nineteenth-century dramas: "Oh, oh, oh! Six o'clock and the master not home yet. Pray God nothing serious has happened to him crossing the Hudson River." She laments the excessive cold and the general mess everything is in, and cannot understand why the house hasn't fallen down long ago. At this point a fragment of the right wall leans precariously over, as though to intrude the shakiness of the stage setting into the general shakiness of the human condition. Throughout the play Wilder will use these devices, presenting the action and then reminding us in various ways that it is only a play, not reality at all. But there will be times that the actors become so involved in the reality of what they are doing that they will forget their real identities and show antagonisms they are supposed to be feeling only as *dramatis personae.* Taking a further cue from Pirandello, Wilder gives the maid a few observations concerning the author, who "hasn't made up his silly mind as to whether we're all living back in caves or in New Jersey today, and that's the way it is all the way through." (The Director in Pirandello's *Six Characters in Search of an Author* complains that he is rehearsing a play by Pirandello called *Mixing It Up,* which nobody can understand.)

Sabina continues to feed the audience information, half in the parodic style she has been using and half to try to explain the situation. The Antrobus family (the Greek word for man is *anthropos*) consists of two children, Henry and Gladys, in addition to the parents. Henry is a "real, clean-cut American boy." But Henry, Sabina tells us, can hit anything when he has a stone in his hand. So the Henry of the play is also the Cain of the Bible.

Sabina goes on lamenting the state of the world, making reference to the fact that "a few years ago we came through the depression by the skin of our teeth! One more tight squeeze like that and where will we all be?" This is a line that needs a response from another actor, but when he doesn't give it Sabina speaks the line again, desperately waiting for the other actor to pick up his cue. Then she bursts into tears, denounces the play and the fate that has reduced her to acting in such trash, and bemoans the old days of *Smilin' Through* and *Peg o' My Heart,* when plays were nice and cheerful. She herself (her real name is Miss Somerset) has appeared in *The Barretts of Wimpole Street* and *Rain* (further references to theatrical carpentry rather than great drama) and begins her speech again.

She and Mrs. Antrobus understand each other. For Sabina (whose history goes back to the rape of the Sabine Women) is also the daughter of Lilith, the temptress of the Bible with whom Mr. Antrobus has once fallen in love. Eventually she lost her place in his home and was demoted to maid. The Eternal Feminine, she is a symbol of those who love only comfort and ease: they can be bought for the simplest luxuries. And Mrs. Antrobus sums her up: "Always throwing up the sponge, Sabina . . . . But give you a new hat—or a plate of ice cream—or a ticket to the movies, and you want to

live forever." If Mrs. Antrobus knows the truth about
Sabina, the reverse is also true. Sabina says of Mrs.
Antrobus, "You don't care whether we live or die; all
you care about is [your] children. If it would be any
benefit to them you'd be glad to see us all stretched and
dead." Sabina, or sensual pleasure, taunts Mrs. Antrobus with the knowledge that she, Sabina, inspired
Mr. Antrobus to invent the alphabet, but Mrs. Antrobus
is not impressed. Sabina was demoted because she let
the fire go out; Mrs. Antrobus keeps the home fires
burning.

In the midst of all this weaving back and forth into the
past and present (with a quick eye on the future), using
the threads of Biblical allusions, Roman history, and
American sources, two creatures of the Ice Age, a
Dinosaur and a Mammoth, try to come in, for they are
very cold in the subzero temperature of August. (Wilder's admiration for André Obey's *Noé* is quite apparent
here, for the French dramatist had made ample use of
actors in animal costumes who were part of the story of
Noah and the Flood.) In the middle of this intrusion, in
turn, Sabina breaks off and remarks that she wishes it
were eleven o'clock and the silly play over. Her major
function in the comedy is to break the action on stage
and to remind the spectator of its illusionary quality.
Just before Mr. Antrobus returns home he sends a
telegram announcing that he has discovered something
new about numbers: "ten tens make hundred."
Antrobus-Adam, Man, the source of knowledge, of
language, of mathematics, advises his family by telegram to fight the cold and keep warm by burning

everything—except Shakespeare. Mrs. Antrobus, Eve–
Earth Goddess, knows better than that: "I'd burn ten
Shakespeares to prevent a child of mine from having
one cold in the head." She lends the Telegraph Boy a
needle (over Sabina's protests, for there are only two
left), so that his wife may sew some warm clothes; and to
comfort him because of his fear of the cold in August,
she advises, "Just keep as warm as you can. And don't let
your wife and children see that you're worried."

Throughout the play Mr. and Mrs. Antrobus worry
about Henry, wondering whether he has hit someone
seriously with a stone. He is constantly warned by his
mother to keep the hair brushed over his forehead so
that the scar on it may not be seen. As the first act
concludes, the ice threatens to engulf the entire world,
and when refugees knock at the door to seek protection
Mrs. Antrobus does not want to take them in; her first
instinct is to save her own family. But Mr. Antrobus
recognizes his duty to mankind and gives them shelter.
They are neighbors, but their names are Judge Moses,
Homer, and the nine Miss Muses. Both religion and
literature are thus saved, while Sabina calls out to the
audience to pass up chairs from the auditorium and
save the human race. The ushers move back and forth
between the stage and the orchestra, this time turning
illusion into reality.

The first act, or Ice Age, may be called the geological
division. The disasters are physical ones caused largely
by nature. The second act, on the boardwalk at Atlantic
City, involves the Flood; since in this act Mr. Antrobus
contemplates abandoning his wife for Sabina, who is

now not a maid but a beauty-contest winner named Miss Fairweather (the name indicates she functions best when there are no problems), he has committed a moral transgression. The disaster has moved from external to internal causes. Interestingly enough, when he announces to Mrs. Antrobus that he is leaving her, she rejects the idea that he can forsake either her or his responsibilities to his fellows in this new crisis. And she makes what is probably Wilder's definitive remark about human obligations:

> I didn't marry you because you were perfect. I didn't even marry you because I loved you. I married you because you gave me a promise. [*She takes off her ring and looks at it.*] That promise made up for your faults. And the promise I gave you made up for mine. Two imperfect people got married and it was the promise that made the marriage . . . . And when our children were growing up, it wasn't a house that protected them; and it wasn't our love, that protected them—it was that promise.

And the breaking of the promise has shattering implications, for their daughter, Gladys, finding attraction in sin, though she is as yet guiltless, appears wearing a pair of scarlet stockings that symbolize the Fall. Her father's horror when he understands the bad example he has set is exceeded only by his reaction to the news over the loudspeaker that the Flood is rising higher and higher.

Recalled to his sense of duty, Antrobus renounces Sabina and self, and moves to rescue his family as the act concludes. Its theme has been echoed earlier by the gaudy Fortune Teller; preposterous fraud though she is, Wilder gives her some characteristic lines:

> You know as well as I do what's coming. Rain. Rain. Rain in floods. The deluge. But first you'll see shameful things—shameful things. Some of you will be saying:"Let him drown. He's not worth saving. Give the whole thing up." I can see it in your faces. But you're wrong. Keep your doubts and despairs to yourself. Again there'll be the narrow escape. The survival of a handful. From destruction—total destruction.

The third act, in contrast again, is historical; this time the disasters have been caused by war, which has just ended when the act begins. The chaos of the world after such a calamity is reflected in the backstage difficulties: seven of the actors have fallen ill, presumably of food poisoning, and the wardrobe mistress and others working on the crew will have to substitute. As it turns out, the understudies have minor roles in terms of lines, but major roles in terms of ideas: Planets, Hours, the same symbols Wilder had used in "Pullman Car Hiawatha," make their appearance. Spinoza, the Ninth Hour, warns man of the confusion in the world outside; Plato, the Tenth Hour, warns of the chaos within the human heart; Aristotle, the Eleventh Hour, praises the beauty of reason. And at twelve, the Book of Genesis begins. The elements that survive are books and faith, or humanism and theology. And it is fitting that Genesis should begin the new day, one second after midnight, marking the Alpha and Omega of the human story. It is also significant that the "regular" actors could not play their parts, yet the substitutes were easy to find, for *everyone* can perform such a function in time of need; it requires no special talents.

The major conflict, such as it exists in this play, is concentrated in the third act, when Henry suddenly emerges in all his evil. He has not only killed his brother (Mrs. Antrobus weeps when a stranger says he thought she had *two* sons), he is wickedness personified. Sabina is quick to realize that he is the enemy. And Henry proves his nature in committing acts that Wilder surely equated with the Nazism that was rampaging across the world. He says, "The first thing to do is burn up those old books [his father's]; it's the ideas he gets out of those old books that . . . makes the whole world so you can't live in it." Sabina urges him to be more lovable; but Henry rejects love (he is the opposite of all the people who found the answer to life in *The Bridge of San Luis Rey*), shouting that he doesn't want anyone to love him.

> Tear everything down. I don't care what you smash . . . . You don't have to think I'm any relation of yours. I haven't got any father or any mother, or brothers or sisters. And I don't want any. And what's more I haven't got anybody over me; and I never will have. I'm alone, and that's all I want to be: alone.

But his is not the loneliness of the perceptive, sensitive human being who recognizes the difficulty of communication; it is the loneliness of the mind that removes itself from the race. Dolly Levi of *The Matchmaker* finds her purpose by rejoining the world; Henry renounces it. And Henry tells his father how he will make the world of the future—by repression of others. This is his father's answer (and Wilder's):

> How can you make a world for people to live in, unless you've first put order in yourself? Mark my words: I shall continue fighting you until my last breath as long as you mix up your idea of liberty with your idea of hogging everything for yourself. I shall have no pity on you. I shall pursue you to the far corners of the earth. You and I want the same thing; but until you think of it as something that everyone has a right to, you are my deadly enemy and I will destroy you.

As the anger builds between the two, Sabina interrupts and begs them not to play out the scene, reminding them of what happened the last time. And now, not Henry the character but Henry the actor recalls his hatred for his father and his own unhappy boyhood, which he has projected into his role. He remembers being hated by his classmates in high school and his feeling of emptiness. And he feels "it's as though you have to kill somebody else so as not to end up killing yourself." Antrobus responds to him now also in his own personality, as an actor on stage, and muses, "It's not wholly his [Henry's] fault . . . it's my fault, too. He wouldn't feel that way unless there were something in me that reminded him of all that." And Henry, grateful for this understanding, leaves the stage, promising not to forget himself too much in the role on future nights.

Sabina, though not wicked or evil, is greedy and

self-serving. She tries to make a little profit out of a situation—anything for comfort. Her complaint:

> I didn't make this war. I didn't ask for it. And, in my opinion, after anybody's gone through what we've gone through, they have a right to grab what they can find . . . . Oh, the world's an awful place, and you know it is. I used to think something could be done about it: but I know better now. I hate it. I hate it.

Antrobus, though driven to depair himself and not really anxious to do anything about saving the world a third time (the Ice Age and the Flood were quite enough), knows that all the same he has to keep trying. He explains to his wife:

> Now I remember what three things always went together when I was able to see things most clearly: three things. Three things. The voice of the people in their confusion and their need. And the thought of you and the children and this house. . . . And . . . my books!

Books can rebuild the world, he believes:

> Oh, I've never forgotten for long at a time that living is struggle. I know that every good and excellent thing in the world stands moment by moment on the razor-edge of danger and must be fought for— whether it's a field, or a home, or a country. All I ask is the chance to build new worlds and God has always given us that. And has given us [*opening the book*] voices to guide us; and the memory of our

mistakes to warn us . . . . We've come a long ways.
We've learned. We're learning. And the steps of our
journey are marked for us here [*he turns the leaves of
the book*].

This is the Holy Trinity for Antrobus: memory (of past
experiences), learning (humanism), and faith (in God,
Nature, Universal Mind—in short, a Creator).

For the last scene of the play the Hours and the Book
of Genesis guard the stage, while the figure of Henry
broods in the background; then everything vanishes
with the stroke of the bell and Sabina begins the same
speech with which she started the play, interrupting
herself to tell the audience they can go home now. "The
end of this play isn't written yet. Mr. and Mrs. Antrobus! Their heads are full of plans and they're as
confident as the first day they began."

The Skin of Our Teeth is a curious mixture of diverse
elements. Though some critics have gone so far as to say
Wilder plagiarized from *Finnegans Wake,* Joyce, after
all, employed the circular theory of time after he, in
turn, had taken it from the Italian philosopher Giam-
battista Vico. Édouard Dujardin in his novel *Le Rétour
Éternel* ("The Eternal Return") had also portrayed the
survival of humanity in the story of a family that had
undergone terrible sacrifices at different ages of history.
Rather than accusing Wilder of plagiarism, it would be
more accurate to say that he had taken a great many
elements from his earlier plays. Thus Mrs. Antrobus is
certainly a development of Mrs. Kirby in "The Happy
Journey to Trenton and Camden"—the Eternal

Mother-Wife. The constant speeches to the audience by the characters coming down stage and facing front recall the technique of *The Matchmaker,* which also parodied the conventions of the old-fashioned box-shaped set. The idea of time itself and man moving in and out of it had already been demonstrated in *Our Town.* And Mr. Antrobus, in the end, is no H. C. Earwicker (the hero of *Finnegans Wake*): he is too incurably American, in his faith, his optimism, and his sense of mission to be anything but another version of George Brush. Moreover, like everything else Wilder wrote, *The Skin of Our Teeth* is highly objective. With such a disjointed and open technique as he uses the tone is usually highly subjective, introspective, full of free association, as in the plays of August Strindberg (or the films of Ingmar Bergman): such dramas always sound deeply personal and autobiographical. But Wilder's comedy, while it expresses his philosophy, has nothing personally revealing about it: we learn everything we have to know by what the characters tell each other and the audience candidly and boldly. There is no feeling of an interior monologue here, probably because Wilder is too intellectual in his approach to submerge his ideas in emotional outpourings.

The Skin of Our Teeth carries the author's primary message that humanity can, must, and will triumph over adversity. But in this play Wilder also goes one step further in his explorations and examines in greater detail than usual the nature of evil itself. From where did it come? And why? The second question has already been answered for us, if indirectly: Wilder seems to

suggest that evil almost *has* to be present as an in-
gredient of life in order for mankind to conquer it. But
the answer to the first question proves to be the weakest
portion of the play.

Although *The Skin of Our Teeth* is both amusing and
technically effective, although it divorces itself from the
tired concept of drama as a series of confrontations
between opposing forces (after all, Chekhov did not
believe much in confrontations and he managed to be
dramatic enough) and is inventive about what is substi-
tuted, the play fails because it attempts to define the
problem of evil in terms of the character of Henry. If he
is Cain and the symbol of wickedness, who really created
him: how did he—Evil—originate?

Mr. Antrobus seems to feel that Henry's wickedness
stems from being misunderstood: there is no other
explanation for the scene when Henry suddenly becomes an unhappy actor who was badly treated by his
friends. We are told that Henry would be able to
understand the alphabet, which his father invented, if it
were a little simpler—but that, too, is a simplification.
Moreover, it is not Henry's act but the coming of the
Flood that is timed to accompany the sins of Mr.
Antrobus: his wrongdoing consists of wishing to abandon his family—that is, his human responsibility—but
his transgressions seem too petty for the deluge that will
engulf everyone. And the Ice Age of the first act, for
which no one is to blame, for no moral lapse has been
witnessed—how is that explained? Wilder simply has
not the kind of talent to make evil seem real, and
consequently the "dark" side of his moon never seems

very dark. He is more at home in chronicling "Man's spiral progress and his progression through trial and error." He understands the anthropological or the ethical man a good deal more than the political one. That is why *Our Town* is more successful than *The Skin of Our Teeth.* Wilder himself has noted that the latter play is most successful when the world looks gloomy— one reason perhaps for its extraordinary success in Germany after the war. Its first production in America baffled some audiences and charmed others; when it was revived recently, its technique was no longer as startling as it had been almost thirty years before, and its philosophy was considered a bit too cheerful. For whatever reason one chooses to supply, it has always been disliked by the French, who are perhaps cynics by profession.

Between 1942 and 1948 Wilder served his country. Stationed in Europe and Africa, he had an opportunity to see some of the uglier aspects of this new conflagration and was touched by it in a way he had never been touched by America's depression in 1929–1930. He became interested in the writings of Søren Kierkegaard, considered by some to be the founder of modern existentialism; more important still, he became a close friend of Jean-Paul Sartre, former professor of philosophy, member of the resistance movement to overthrow Nazi rule in France, novelist and playwright, and the leader of the intellectual life of Paris in the 1940's. Wilder translated Sartre's play *The Victors* for a 1948 production in New York, shortly before publishing his next novel of the same year, *The Ides of March.* Just as

Obey had interested him enough to make him translate *Lucrèce* and later use some of Obey's ideas in his own play, so Sartre's thinking had a strong influence on the tone of *The Ides of March,* which remains the most skeptical work Wilder ever produced.

Sartre's play about the resistance, *The Victors,* is also a study in survival. It concerns Free French fighters, partisans of General de Gaulle who fought against the surrender of France to the Germans. These brave men and women have been captured and tortured in order to make them reveal the names of their other comrades. Every conceivable kind of torment is tried on them: physical, mental, spiritual. One of them, a girl, is raped repeatedly; she remains silent about the sixty Frenchmen who will die if their identities are known. Another victim is a fifteen-year-old boy who cries, "Help! I don't want to die here, not in this blackness. I'm fifteen, let me live. Don't kill me in the dark." The other prisoners, knowing the boy will break under his agony, strangle him quickly to put him out of his anguish.

The leader of the group decides he will tell their captors what they want to know, hoping to save the prisoners and at the same time send the collaborationists out on a false trail. But the girl doesn't want him even to *seem* to have yielded: she wants to be shot. He asks her what the point is in dying: "If you die today, the picture will be completed. But if you live . . . then nothing will be settled. It's by your whole life that your individual acts will be judged. If you let yourself be shot while there's still work for you to do, nothing will be more senseless than your death." Sartre's study of how men apply their philosophy to everyday life is the basis of this, as of his other, plays. The questions he raised in *The Victors* crop up, if somewhat disguised because of setting and subject, in *The Ides of March.*

The novel was dedicated to two of Wilder's friends: Lauro de Bosis, an Italian poet who died in the struggle against Mussolini; and Edward Sheldon, an American playwright who, while still young and at the height of his power and popularity, suffered a stroke that left him crippled and blind for twenty years before his death. It was the courage of both these men that inspired the characterization of two figures in the book: the Roman poet Catullus and Caesar's lifelong friend, Lucius Mamilius Turrinus, like Sheldon a hopeless cripple. In *Our Town* the Stage Manager tells Emily that maybe the poets and saints understand a little about the mystery of life: in *The Ides of March* Catullus, tormented by unrequited love, turns his agony into magnificent lyrics; while Turrinus, seen only through the eyes of Caesar, helps the great statesman to formulate some philosophy of life through the wisdom he himself has learned through physical suffering.

Although the book aims at verisimilitude, Wilder tells us in the foreword that he has imagined a great deal of the material, altered historical facts, shifted dates, and generally arranged events in order to create the effects he wanted. The background is authentic up to a point; when artistic demands become more important, they dictate what is to occur. To add to the "realism" of the novel, Wilder introduces customs, ceremonies, activities, and other details of the local scene, so that ancient

Rome may be understood, like the modern world, by the daily routine of its citizens—the same technique he had employed before (in *Our Town*) in juxtaposing the trivial with the lofty, the unessential with the significant. The means he uses to achieve his purpose take the form of seemingly factual sources; thus bits and pieces of biography, diaries, letters, confidential police reports, journals, news items of the day—in short, documents alone—serve to tell the story that culminates in the assassination of Julius Caesar. A number of the characters in the novel are introduced by the observations of others; sometimes the reader learns about them from their own revelations. What Wilder achieves here is a kind of editorial effect, as though he had discovered these "authentic" commentaries written by different hands and bound them together in one book, as though a scholar had put together past history in the same manner as an archaeologist would restore the column of a temple. This is the only Wilder novel in which the all-seeing author-narrator does not appear in order to interrupt or philosophize; each character contributes his own view of life to the reader, who makes a final judgment.

In French poet and dramatist Paul Claudel's play *Christophe Colombe,* two different actors play the part of Columbus, one representing the explorer as he lived in fifteenth-century Spain, the other representing Columbus as discussed in the history books. By shifting back and forth in time in *The Ides of March,* Wilder gives us access not only to documents contemporary with Caesar but also makes mention of Caesar's character as seen a century later by a distinguished Roman historian. (The technique is still that of *The Skin of Our Teeth,* adapted to narrative form.) The novel is arranged in an arbitrary yet perfectly natural way. It is divided into four parts: each book covers the same principal events; each starts a little earlier and each ends a little later, giving the effect of overlap. The novel concentrates on the month of September in 45 B.C.; it returns to the past by one month and then moves to the future by six months. It ends with the events of March 15, 44 B.C., when Caesar was stabbed to death. Although the story concerns ancient Rome, the parallels with the modern world are clear and are heightened by the unusual time device Wilder uses; as one book ends and the same story is taken up again from another point of view and another point in time in another book, the reader has the sensation of watching a weaving process. The threads are taken up and worked in one way; others then are subjected to the same treatment. At first no design is apparent, but by the time the novel has concluded, the total picture—or pattern—is there. *The Ides of March,* as sheer technique, is the most brilliant, original, and inventive work of Wilder's entire career.

The book is different from his other work in still another way: its theme is power and the philosophy that animates dictators and their enemies. Drawing on the historical fact of the conspiracy against Caesar and his assassination, Wilder is able, for the first time, to ponder the question of man as seen in a context that is less ethical or anthropological and more political in scope. This aspect of *The Skin of Our Teeth* was touched upon rather ineffectively in its third act; here it occupies the center of the author's intention. In the character of Caesar Wilder traces the change in Rome from republic to gradual empire and the relationship between a ruler and his people.

On the whole, Wilder has always been less interested in character than in ideas: one or two of his people in *The Bridge of San Luis Rey* and George Brush in *Heaven's My Destination* are the only creations that are memorable as human beings. In *The Ides of March,* however, the major and several minor characters have vividness and conviction. As a result, the novel has a richness and a complexity lacking in Wilder's other books.

Julius Caesar, naturally, dominates the action. But we see Caesar in many guises. He is a sensual man, the lover of Cleopatra, the man who seizes the joys of today since there may be no tomorrow. He is a philosophical man, forever asking himself (and occasionally others) the meaning of life and the reason for its mystery. He is a rational man, despising portents and omens and auguries as superstition that destroys religion. He sees one of his functions in the world as that of teacher: he wants to educate the people so that they may understand the art of government. Even his silly young wife Pompeia is a subject for his passionate pedagogy, though with her he fails, for only when it is too late does he realize that not everyone is a learner. That, too, takes a special grace. He is a lover of art and a respecter of genius; hence, although the poet Catullus hates him and attacks him in verse, Caesar both admires and forgives him. He despises apathy, the philosophy of *Che sera,*

sera, yet he does not know how to rouse the people and make them shake it off. (There is more than an echo here of the contempt expressed by Sartre in his play *The Flies* for those who shrug their shoulders and shuffle off responsibility.) Caesar despises most of all those who squander their heritage, like the Lady Clodia, Catullus' beloved. He is a moral man who believes "we cannot be aware of our minds save under responsibility." And he is a realist: "Man is alone in a world in which no voices were heard other than his own, a world neither friendly nor unfriendly save as he made it so."

Existentialism has placed heavy emphasis on this loneliness in terms of its alienated heroes. To an extent, Caesar may be called one too. But whereas the existentialist heroes also look with disgust upon the world (Hamlet is a perfect example) and suffer from boredom and anxiety, Caesar is free of these pressures. Physically he is harassed by epilepsy, yet it is during these attacks of his illness that he has visions which, he believes, lead him to the truth about life; power, love, and poetry are the other sources of illumination. Because of this difference from other existentialist heroes, Caesar is willing to accept the mystery of life. He believes that good and evil are but links in a chain, that a law does operate though we do not understand it. His wry comment on man's pursuit for a meaning to life shows a subtle appreciation of the hold religion, as a mystery, has over us: "If the gods were not so hidden we would not peer so hard to find them."

Most striking of all, Wilder's Caesar is a man with a supreme understanding of irony—not the gentle brand that Wilder usually used. There are times when Caesar's aphorisms sound more like those of the French essayist and wit La Rochefoucauld: at one point, recalling his youth, Caesar notes: "I once believed that burning intensity in the mind can bring a message from an indifferent loved one . . . and that sheer indignation can halt the triumphs of an enemy." But he knows now that "Hope has never changed tomorrow's weather." He looks upon those who do not foresee their death as children, and he knows that "only those who have grasped their non-being are capable of praising the sunlight." His skepticism leads him to observe, when he comforts Catullus, that "the universe goes its mighty way and there is very little we can do to modify it." And he thinks there is probably no meaning to life because he prefers a world where there is none, save for what we give it. And finally, he believes that there is no limit to wisdom: "where there is an unknowable there is promise." He adds, "On the meaningless I choose to press a meaning and in the wastes of the Unknowable I choose to be known."

But this Caesar is the one who writes letters to his friend; the Caesar the reader sees through the letters of others is quite a different man. The Lady Clodia hates him and spreads scandal about him; Brutus, played upon by his unscrupulous mother, regards him as a tyrant (his mother suggests that Caesar hates Brutus because the latter is really Caesar's illegitimate son). Caesar's wife, Pompeia, looks on him as a bit of an elderly bore always trying to instruct and uplift her. Catullus looks upon him as a hypocrite. Saddest of all, the conspirators, bound together by their envy and hate, look upon him as a man whose political ideas are too dangerous—not because he wishes to be dictator, but because he has some radical notion about educating people politically. He is different from them, for he sees power as a way of accepting his responsibilities, not as a means for self-indulgence. And they do not understand this concept. They murder him because his vision of life is so unorthodox in their eyes; and the final absurdity is that he, the strongest figure in Rome in the sense of a man possessing moral convictions, is slain by the weakest man in Rome, who has no convictions at all—Brutus. Caesar sees that his fellow-Romans have become skilled in avoiding commitment. He, on the other hand, is willing to arrive at a decision and sustain it. "Everyone," he notes, "wants liberty; everyone avoids its consequences." In effect, he becomes The Man Who Must Die. When we have pieced together this multifaceted character, we can understand why Wilder's epigraph to the book is an interpretation of two lines from Goethe's *Faust:* "Out of man's recognition in fear and awe that there is an Unknowable comes all that is best in the explorations of his mind,—even though that recognition is often misled into superstition, enslavement, and overconfidence."

Equally unforgettable is Lady Clodia, as much as anyone in this book the embodiment of evil. She had been corrupted by her uncle at the age of twelve and has, ever afterward, determined to wreak her revenge on the human race—particularly on men. She has a superb mind as well as great beauty; and it pleases her fancy to dangle one of Rome's greatest poets, Catullus, on a hook, causing him to write, "I love you and I hate you." The reader is already familiar with Wilder's examination of unrequited love in all its various forms, from *The Cabala* on; but the anguish of Catullus seems far more real than that of other characters Wilder has drawn who are afflicted with the same disease. Was it the *poet's* anguish, one wonders, as he wrote his immortal lyrics, that caught Wilder's imagination strongly enough to give reality to the pain?

Clodia's unsavory reputation—she and her brother were probably lovers—seems to have come about through her own self-hatred. If she hates Caesar, it is because she is also in love with him and he has rejected her. Not because of her "immorality," but because of her love of evil for its own sake. She is the most successful "wicked" character Wilder has ever drawn. Because she knows she cannot touch Caesar, she attempts to damage him through his wife: her brother, who is in a shadowy way almost as depraved as she, pursues Pompeia with protestations of love, and that foolish woman, not recognizing that she is a cat's-paw in the game, is flattered. The final evil Clodia commits is to arrange with Pompeia to smuggle her brother, disguised as a woman, into the temple during the rites of the Bona Dea; by involving Pompeia in a sacrilegious plot she can be sure that some of the mud will rub off on Pompeia's husband—the great Caesar—since the offense is heavily punishable by law. It is the mockery of faith and the frivolity of mind that cannot comprehend Infinity, much more than the possible act of infidelity by

his wife, that Caesar abhors. He divorces Pompeia: he
has tried to instruct her; with her, he has failed as a
teacher. Her levity has affected him as a devout Catholic
might be affected seeing the Sacrament taken from its
place and passed around with peanuts at the cocktail
hour.

Clodia uses other ways to strike at Caesar; since he is
fond of Marc Antony, who has had the love of a Greek
actress, Cytheris, for fifteen years, Clodia arranges to
destroy the affair. Cytheris reminds the reader of *The
Woman of Andros* in her grace of spirit and her artistic
sensitivity; it is natural that both Caesar and Turrinus
should be her friends. By making Cytheris wretched,
Clodia hopes to sadden Caesar. She is determined to
make him react to her existence in some way, even if it is
to hate her. And so Clodia helps Marc Antony to
ensnare the magnificent Queen of Egypt, and he and
Cleopatra become lovers. Clodia goes further. She
initiates a plan whereby chain letters are circulated
against Caesar (Wilder took this idea from a similar plot
against Mussolini, suggested by George Bernard Shaw)
and scurrilous slanders are whispered. But she is not
particularly successful. Even Catullus is reconciled to
Caesar before the poet dies: Clodia loses her last par-
tisan.

The character of Clodia seems also to have some
foundation in fact. Glenway Wescott recalls a story
Wilder once told him of a beautiful New York society
girl who had become a successful actress and later fell in
love with a man who never cared deeply for her. One
day she phoned him and threatened to take her life,

whereupon he tried to comfort her but on the whole discounted her warnings. That evening she committed suicide. Wilder told Wescott that he felt much more sympathy for the man than for the girl who had died—a reaction that puzzled Wilder's friend. Later, when reading *The Ides of March,* Wescott suddenly understood Wilder's point of view, for Caesar explains that he has lost patience with Clodia, who

> persistently loved him for years, while trailing a wrecked life around behind her, compensating for a tragic misfortune in her childhood by nonstop mischievousness and cruelty ever since, acquitting herself of every charge but never ceasing to feel guilty, exhibiting herself as the victim, the victim, whatever has happened, re-erecting a sacrificial altar at every turn and exhibiting herself on it, striking attitudes on it, victimizing herself if no one else is available to do it for her.

It is the harshest page Wilder has ever written, and one of the profoundest.

But if from the beginning Caesar was destined to fall and to be brought to the dust by a weak and nervous conspirator like Brutus, from the beginning Clodia was destined to be a link in the chain of the conspiracy. It is she who encourages the conspirators; it is she who glories in the fact that she can warn and so save Caesar, that she has in effect the power of life and death over him. In a moment of compunction she calls and tells him to avoid going out on the fatal day; she confesses her knowledge of the plot. But with an uncanny wisdom

Caesar, looking at her, has an instant picture of her as an old woman sitting by the fire and telling people how she saved the state. Even her act of atonement is tainted; whether she is telling the truth about the plot or not is of no importance. He rejects her advice because of the motive for it. It is a short, tightly compressed, brilliantly written scene, that moment of instant recognition between the two of them, each knowing the heart of the other, neither speaking—a genuine Chekhov moment.

Caesar half knows that he will die if he leaves for the Forum, but he knows also that even if he does not go that day his death cannot be averted for long. He has seen more clearly than his fellows—and death is the price he must pay. The last letter but one in the book is written by his third wife, Calpurnia, to her sister. It is a simple note explaining her worry about her husband, who has planned to go to the Senate on the Ides of March. She is ashamed of her fears but can't explain them and hopes all will go well. The letter that follows hers, the last in the book, is taken from an account (authentic) by the historian Suetonius in *The Lives of the Caesars;* it is a bald recital of the murder, the twenty-three stab wounds, and the diagnosis by the physician that only the second one would have proved fatal. The dry manner of the telling, in sharp contrast to the emotional tone of the previous letter written by a frightened wife, makes the death of Caesar all the more shattering; the extreme objectivity is the element that rouses a subjective response in the reader. As Wilder has drawn it, the death of Julius Caesar becomes high tragedy.

Catullus remains the bridge between Caesar and Clodia. He loves Clodia, Clodia loves Caesar, Caesar loves Catullus' art. Caesar's admiration springs from his belief that great poets can gaze at all of life and find harmony, and in the lyrics that Catullus composes Caesar finds exactly that. Interestingly enough, the orator Cicero despises Catullus, accusing him of self-indulgence, of wearing his heart on his sleeve. Cicero, as a member of the older generation, has little sympathy with the young, and most of his ill-natured comments directed against Catullus suggest not only jealousy but a total unawareness of a different life style.

During a banquet scene, when someone asks, "Where does poetry come from?" and the answer is varied (the gods give it to the poet; it is drawn from the anguish of those who want a better world—this is Clodia's explanation), Catullus tries to explain by quoting the legend of Alcestis, who rejects marriage to become a priestess of Apollo at Delphi. Although Admetus loves her, he lets her go. The seer Tiresias announces that Apollo is coming to live in the palace for a year; he will take his place as one of the herdsmen. As there are five of them, no one knows which is Apollo. Are there, in fact, any gods at all, or is the whole idea a myth? Before Catullus can finish the story or provide an answer at the banquet, Caesar has an epileptic attack; the story is interrupted and never finished. But because Catullus sees Caesar's agony and the loneliness of his spirit, he can no longer hate him as he used to because of Clodia.

By removing hate from Catullus, though at the expense of Caesar's well-being and dignity, by touching

him with pity for the fallen statesman, Wilder has
perhaps supplied the answer indirectly about the existence of the gods. It seems fitting that when Catullus
himself is dying, Caesar should sit beside him and
comfort him. When Catullus cries that he has wasted his
life and his song for the favors of a harlot, Caesar
reminds him of Sophocles' words in *Oedipus at Colonus*
concerning death. It is the poet who gives meaning to
experience.

Love in all its aspects is explored in this novel: the
perverse kind between Catullus and Clodia (although
Wilder does not stress the point, the sado-masochistic
relationship of the couple is clear enough), which is not
only the poet's torment but his glory, since it supplies
the inspiration for his best verse; the self-sacrificing
kind that Cytheris feels for Marc Antony; the possessive
kind, which Clodia feels for Caesar. Above it all, the
friendship of Caesar for his maimed friend Turrinus.
Whatever the reader learns about him comes from the
letters Caesar writes; Wilder does not give any record of
the letters Turrinus sent in exchange.

The two men had been close friends in their youth
and had seen service together. When Turrinus was
captured by the Belgians and would not inform against
Caesar, he was put to the torture: his ears were cropped,
his eyes put out, his body mutilated, an arm and a leg
cut off. Caesar rescued him, risking annihilation in the
process; and ever since that time Turrinus has lived in
seclusion on the island of Capri, visited only by Caesar
and the Greek actress Cytheris. It is only he to whom
Caesar can pour out his heart: cold, objective, self-

sufficient to the rest of the world as Caesar seems, it is from these letters to his friend that we draw a picture of the "real" Caesar. Turrinus' capacity for living uncomplainingly, his mental faculties still unimpaired, his understanding of Caesar's ideas and dreams, his remoteness from the world because of his physical state—all these conditions make him the ideal sounding board for Caesar's thoughts. Just as Mrs. Newsome in Henry James's *The Ambassadors* never appears in the book yet is the mainspring of the action, so Turrinus, forever invisible to us behind the walls of his villa, is the reason for the correspondence—and the novel.

As a means of drawing Caesar still further into the stream of future time, there is an ironical passage taken from a document by the Roman writer Pliny about a century after Caesar's death: a religious sect, devoted to the cult of some obscure Mysteries, robbed and mutilated Caesar's corpse and buried the pieces in different parts of the city as a means of preserving the safety of Rome. So Julius Caesar—destroyed by those who were limited in vision, reactionary in attitude (like the people who hate Chrysis in *The Woman of Andros*), weak in spine, small in nature, proclaimed a tyrant by those who slew him—became in the end a god. Thus are myth and legend born.

The novel is, more than his other works of fiction, Wilder's most dramatic narrative—that is, it shows the effect of the years he had spent in the theater before writing it. As we read the letters written by the different characters, we can hear their "voices," almost like stage dialogue. The mischievous and sumptuous Cleopatra,

worried about her "image" and her "rights"; the fussy
Roman ladies and their perpetual gossip; the great
Cicero, ill-humored and witty; the police spies, ineffec-
tually sniffing out plots—all are realized in a manner
that contradicts Wilder's belief in outline-portraits. All
are more concrete, more "visible"—qualities he had to
provide for the stage in some degree in order to
particularize his ideas.

Wilder tells us that *The Ides of March* can be said "to be
written under the sign of Kierkegaard." Caesar, as an
existentialist hero, a lonely dreamer in an alien world,
but a man of action who shapes his city, is the result of
Wilder's interest in the Danish philosopher. Coupled
with it is Sartre's atheism—though in Wilder it goes no
further than a kind of agnosticism, a polite "I don't
know"—and his exploration of evil and its place in the
scheme of things. Clearly, World War II and its after-
math, wherein horrors were not necessarily perpetrated
on a scale unknown to history but certainly were never
so well publicized before, could no longer be seen by
even the most optimistic as a nasty footnote to the divine
plan. Equally shattering to Wilder must have been the
cultural barbarism of Fascism: the banning and burning
of great literature, art, and music; the smashing of
tradition (young couples were married in Germany by
an official who read to them out of *Mein Kampf* instead
of the Bible); the rending of family ties (children spied
on, and reported, their parents if the latter seemed to be
making treasonable remarks); above all, the mass hys-
teria, the drum-beating, the extravagant emotionalism
of Hitler's rallies (Caesar speaks contemptuously of
people who have "attacks" of religious frenzy).

The Fascists of modern Europe have their counterpart in this novel: they are evil personified, they laugh at honor, despise truth, revel in corruption, betray friends, torment lovers. Between them and Caesar stand the citizens, most of whom go about their business hoping to remain uninvolved, uncommitted. Caesar assumes the burden of responsibility (like Orestes in *The Flies*), choosing to act: spiritual midgets in comparison, they also believe they choose to act, but lacking both moral courage and wisdom, they make the wrong choice. For the Greeks, and for the Elizabethans also, tragedy came through the "flaw" in a man's character that destroyed him. Caesar, although "flawed" simply because he is human, is not brought down because of his weaknesses: he is destroyed by those little minds that cannot act, or else act to no sensible purpose. This is the absurdity of the human condition. Sartre, of course, rejects meaning altogether: one acts or chooses because not to act or choose is not to live. Caesar, as Wilder sees him, still feels conscious of a design, though he accepts the fact that he will never discover it.

Although Wilder was shaken from the position he had held before, a genuine conviction of the essential rightness of things, he did not abandon it entirely. *The Ides of March* is valuable precisely because in it Wilder examined his own faith objectively; the irony that tinged *Heaven's My Destination* (which also provided Wilder with an opportunity for self-mockery) is deeper and more complex in this book and far better able to capture the flavor of life itself. Caesar's torments as he searches for a meaning are real: he is not content to say he has known the "bright and the dark and all is well." A good portion of his letters to his friend Turrinus show a man caught between what is and what ought to be, and the book concentrates on the tensions of Caesar's spiritual journey rather than his arrival at a state of resignation. Although as usual Wilder did not make a direct statement about the world's turmoil in 1948, both it, and the influence of Sartre, produced a change in tone that indicated his response to—not retreat from—the human condition.

While the structure of the book—the same story told from different points of view by different characters—adds a richness to the tone, the style is quite spare, as though Wilder had imitated a Roman historian at his most objective. The simplicity of the writing, therefore, makes a sharp contrast with the complexity of the tale; the almost journalistic flavor is counterpointed by those passages in the novel in which Caesar becomes eloquent or Catullus rhapsodic. As a result, this Caesar seems closest to the real man who was also author of *The Gallic Wars*—crisp, controlled, ironic. Bernard Shaw's Caesar has more wit and charm, but he is only another disguise behind which Shaw himself is lurking. Shakespeare's Caesar is a tired old man waiting to collect his rewards from the Senate. Wilder's Caesar is the stuff of which history is made.

Both in *The Ides of March* and, much earlier, in *The Woman of Andros* Wilder had made mention of the Greek dramatist Euripides and the legend of Alcestis, which Euripides made into a play. From 1948 to 1955, Wilder worked on a version of the classical story until it

was ready to be produced at the Edinburgh Festival in
August 1955, under the direction of Tyrone Guthrie.

In *The Ides* Wilder had tried to study the mind of a
man like Caesar who gave himself to the task of sorting
out religion from superstition and determining whether
he had created his own role as ruler of Rome or whether
Destiny had ordained it and chosen him. How much
free will, in short, did he have? Wilder returned to this
question in *The Alcestiad.*

As Euripides presents the legend, Admetus, King of
Thessaly, falls ill and is doomed to die. The god Apollo,
in the guise of a herdsman, decrees that Admetus will be
spared if a substitute can be found. The King storms,
bribes, pleads, cajoles, but to no avail, for no one wishes
to die. Even his old father, who is so close to death
himself, will not replace his son. Finally, out of her great
love for him, Admetus' queen, Alcestis, takes the sacrifice upon herself. She dies, leaving her husband incon-
solable. But his friend Hercules, half-god, half-man,
jovial and drunken when he makes his first appearance,
goes down to the lower world and wrestles with Death
for Alcestis. In the end he wins and brings her back to
her husband for a happy ending. Euripides, of course,
was interested in exposing the weaknesses of rulers
(Admetus is far from ideal as a human being, especially
in his cruel encounter with his father) and the general
difficulties created by the gods. What we would today
call an antiestablishment playwright's point of view
dominates the tragicomedy. But Wilder saw in the
material certain themes that would carry through the
questions raised in *The Ides.*

Wilder's Hercules, by virtue of being half-god, half-man, is a link with both worlds. He is Admetus' friend and a devoted but platonic admirer of Alcestis. As a man of legendary accomplishments he has performed difficult labors successfully, but like Caesar he is not sure whether he has achieved these feats himself or whether the gods have assisted him. He is most terrified by the thought that someday he will be asked to do the impossible—like rescuing someone from Death—and in that moment he may fail. If he does, he will have proved that his life is purposeless, for demigods should be victorious.

In his book *Fear and Trembling* Kierkegaard had pointed out that when man fears most and yet risks everything, he will regain all that he seems to have lost; the test for Hercules comes when he is indeed forced to wrestle with Death for Alcestis. In his anguish he calls on Apollo, or God, and Apollo helps him to win. Man, cooperating with God, has a chance to triumph, as Hercules demonstrates.

Alcestis, who at the beginning of the play had not wanted to marry at all but to serve Apollo, is the other side of the coin. Whereas Hercules fears the vastness of the universe and questions the existence of the gods, Alcestis fears the commonplace activities of daily life. In *The Ides of March* Caesar remarks, "Our lives are immersed in the trivial; the significant comes to us enwrapped in multitudinous details of the trivial; the trivial has this dignity, that it exists and is omnipresent." Alcestis has yet to learn this truth in order to become a participant in life: when we first meet her she is in

retreat from it because she is repelled by its "ordinariness."

The Alcestiad follows its Greek counterpart in structure: it has as its components three parts and a satyr-
play, "The Drunken Sisters" (what we might today
term a comic curtain-closer). There is a Chorus in the
form of a Watchman, who comments on the occasions
and suggests the Stage Manager of *Our Town*. But
Wilder varies sharply from Euripides in his use of time:
the first act introduces Alcestis before her marriage
when she wishes to serve as a priestess of Apollo; the
second act (which begins where Euripides' play began)
takes place ten years later; and the third act views
Alcestis twenty years after she has been brought back
from the lower world by Hercules.

Euripides had not treated his gods very kindly in most
of his plays: since he detested the superstition that
passed for religion in Athens he lost no opportunity to
debunk it—the first muckraker of ancient times. Correspondingly, Sartre imbued his gods with the same
malice and indifference, since for him God does not
exist, or, as he puts it, "Even if God did exist, he would
not suit my concept of the universe" and so has to be
removed from the scheme of things. Wilder, however,
has never accepted this view; consequently the god of
the play, Apollo, comes quite close to the Christian
concept of deity and is a kind of classical Christ. The
very fact that he comes down to earth to serve as a
herdsman gives him a symbolic link to the story of the
Incarnation.

After Alcestis has announced her decision to serve

Apollo in the first act, the news comes that he will arrive in the form of a herdsman. Balked of her wish, Alcestis accepts Admetus, choosing a love that is human rather than divine. But all the while she keeps looking for a sign that will reassure her of the wonder, the magnificence, the glory of life. In the second act, after she has been married for ten years, she chooses to die for the man she has loved and served in a human sense and who has given her great happiness. Although a number of people are willing to die for the King she knows that it is she who must assume the responsibility, and she resigns herself, like Chrysis in *The Woman of Andros,* to death's inevitability. But, by dying, by renouncing life, she regains it, for Hercules comes to rescue her. She is as necessary to him as he is to her, for she becomes the test he fears and must nevertheless pass if his own life is to have meaning.

Twenty years elapse between the second and the third acts. In that time Admetus has died, a plague has ravaged the land, war has brought about the defeat of the Thessalians and the enslavement of Alcestis. As Death and Apollo opened the play, they come together for the beginning of the last act, during which Apollo predicts, to use the British poet Swinburne's image, "Death lies dead." Epimenes, the only remaining son of Admetus and Alcestis after the tyrant Agis had killed the King and the other two children, returns to Thessaly to avenge his father's death and to claim the throne. Agis now knows the pain of death himself, for his beloved daughter has been stricken by the plague, and he wishes like Hercules to go down to the lower world and rescue her. But Alcestis reminds him that the last bitterness of death is not ceasing to be but rather despair that one has not lived or that one has lived without meaning, foolishly, senselessly. Agis insists that his daughter loved him and so gave meaning to his life, but Alcestis tells him that love is not the only answer, not the only sign. Each human being must find his own. Just as Alcestis began to understand the meaning of life by accepting its shortcomings and resigning herself to its pain, Agis must find his pattern in his own actions, not through his daughter. When Alcestis' son returns to wreak vengeance, Alcestis teaches him that he must not expend his life in idle bitterness but must help to fight the plague. It is then that Apollo gives her the sign she has been looking for so long: *she* is the sign, for she has believed in the face of tragedy and death; and at that moment the plague lifts. She accompanies Apollo on the road to death, but this time it is like the death of Everyman and betokens a resurrection that is part of the Christian victory: there is no more sting to death, there is no triumph for the grave. Having died to herself, she wins immortality.

In contrast to Apollo, the Christ-figure, Death and the seer Tiresias represent the "practical" world. From the first, Death cautions Apollo to leave people alone, for they cannot understand the gods, who only confuse them. He compares the gods to giants in a small room: every time they move about they smash something. He advises Apollo to resign himself to being thought unintelligible: it is the price the gods must pay for creating men free.

Tiresias mocks Apollo in another way. Apollo, he complains, is always talking about love. But he reminds Apollo that everyone would be happier if the gods didn't love men, and men the gods. As a result, one species keeps reaching for the other, and the struggle is too painful, if not downright hopeless. Tiresias' world is like that of the people of Andros or the citizens of Rome: self-satisfaction, complacency, accepting one's limitations—in fact, limiting oneself by accepting them—these are the ways to happiness. Apollo rejects the philosophy, as does Wilder (echoing Robert Browning's Fra Lippo Lippi: "A man's reach should exceed his grasp"); the gods, in causing men to stretch their arms toward the heavens, hold out their own toward the earth. And so another bridge is formed.

The accompanying play, "The Drunken Sisters," further stresses the theme of choice and action by concentrating on Apollo's efforts to make the three Fates alter their decree and allow Admetus to live: Apollo makes them drunk and tricks them into revoking their edict of death against the King. But they insist on one stipulation: they must have a substitute, and that person cannot be an unwilling victim or a slave forced to die for the King. Again, the choice must exist. Therefore free will *does* enter the picture: although events seem unalterable they are still determined by man.

To retain the essential nobility of the idea, Wilder changes Euripides' Admetus from a selfish, ill-mannered despot to a man worthy of Alcestis' sacrifice. He cherishes Apollo; he loves the gods; he is forgiving, tolerant, humane. He understands the maiden Alcestis' craving to serve the god and he waits for her patiently. Another change in Wilder's play is that Pheres, Admetus' disagreeable father in the original, is eliminated—yet another indication of the manner in which Wilder meant the theme to be taken. The result is that no one in the play is truly evil. Agis is a villain, true: he kills Admetus and two of the children, but he redeems himself through love for his daughter and his understanding of pain and death. Alcestis' angry son, who returns breathing the fires of revenge, is also transformed by his mother's example and so reduces the tension of the play. *The Alcestiad* is probably the closest the modern reader can come to a morality play. The characters are personifications; the struggles are achieved invisibly, offstage; the torments are expressed but never dramatized. The rhythm of the play is slow and serene, like frozen music.

Possibly a modern audience simply cannot accept the oversimplification of the medieval world, which *The Alcestiad,* set though it is in antiquity, really represents. The theme appears more moving in the original morality play *Everyman* because everything in that play is childlike and one-dimensional, giving the effect of a twelfth-century woodcut. But a number of the speeches and arguments in *The Alcestiad* are highly modern and sophisticated in their point of view, and its modernity jars with its simple message, "Love one another and be resigned, blessed are those who do not see and yet believe." After the imaginative barbarism and the fiendish devices for torture and extinction of World War II, it is difficult to comprehend a "gentle Jesus, meek and mild," in whom one can hope and trust. But even if one could accept this Gandhi-like resignation, sought also by the German philosopher of modern times, Martin Buber, Wilder's problem is that he has revealed the joys and philosophized about them, but the agonies are kept offstage. Caesar in intellectual torment brings life to *The Ides of March;* Alcestis resigning herself to the bitterness of death seems too remote, too good, too saintlike for ordinary apprehension. And there is no Clodia in this play to offer the contrapuntal theme of evil.

The seeming shift in Wilder's view that marked *The Ides of March* slipped back again into the stance of *The Woman of Andros,* for *The Alcestiad* is just that—a dramatic rendering of his third novel. It was apparent that regardless of his exposure to the ugliness of life and to intellectual assaults on his point of view, Wilder remained constant in his faith. One may quarrel with it, but one must admire its integrity.

Glenway Wescott speaks of a letter written to him by Wilder and dated May 23, 1948, in which Wilder told his friend that for some time he had been seeking a large and fundamental concept and project to work on, adding: "A writer spends his time hunting for his real right subject; that subject which Meredith never found, which Cervantes almost missed, which Henry James caught three times, and so on—and where is mine?" Wilder wondered whether it was possible for a writer to arrive at his principal and final theme "by contemplation or calculation, or must it be heaven-sent? Can one even, by taking thought, preserve oneself from this or that erroneous undertaking or hollow, infertile concept?"

By whatever means artistic inspiration may come, before long Wilder found it in his next project, a cycle of one-act plays having two great parallel and connecting themes: the seven stages of man from babyhood to death, and the seven weaknesses that destroy him. One cycle, then, was to study physical man; the other, moral man. Wilder saw both cycles as a means of stressing the links binding people to each other: he wanted to dramatize "things that repeat and repeat and repeat in the lives of the millions." By using subject matter of such universality, he believed that the creative artist, "by realizing and exteriorizing the public consciousness and conscience, can help everyone." In embarking on this monumental work Wilder saw himself not only as a writer but as a teacher, an inculcator of values.

The group dealing with the seven deadly sins consisted, by 1970, of four one-act plays. "Berniece," representing the sin of pride, was performed in West Berlin in 1957, but was unsuccessful and discarded by Wilder, who has not revised or published it. "Sloth," another of the sins, is also unpublished and has not been produced. It is interesting largely from the standpoint of Wilder's interpretation of this vice: to him the sin of sloth means that one has failed to live life fully, a theme he developed at length in *The Alcestiad.* Gluttony is the subject of his satyr-play "The Drunken Sisters," but at present it is not sure that Wilder will retain it in the cycle. Only "Someone from Assisi" has been produced in America: this one-act play demonstrates the sin of lust.

Explaining in an interview that he was "not interested in the ephemeral—such subjects as the adulteries of dentists," and indicating that he would of necessity return to the freedom of the "play in space" (unlike *The Matchmaker,* which demanded a formal box-set), Wilder continued: "Because we live in the twentieth century, overhung by very real anxiety, we have to use the comic spirit." He did not believe that is was possible to make grave statements that would be "equal to the gravity of the age in which we live."

"Someone from Assisi," together with two one-act plays from the second cycle, "Infancy" and "Childhood," was produced in New York off-Broadway in 1962, at the Bleecker Street Playhouse, Circle-in-the-Square. The structure of the theater was particularly right for the kind of plays Wilder had in mind: its seating arrangement was such that the audience could sit on three sides of the stage, much as they had in Shakespeare's time. This feeling of openness in the physical theater, Wilder believed, would reinforce the effect he was seeking to produce with his plays.

The first play introduces us to St. Francis after he has withdrawn from the world and become a monk. In his youth he had had an affair with a girl whom he afterward abandoned when he decided to renounce the world. Suffering from her rejection, she has finally become mad. When St. Francis meets her many years later, he feels responsible for her suffering and takes it upon himself to provide for her. The play seems more concerned with our commitments to each other than with the sin of lust. In addition, St. Francis has moved so far from his early errors that he is beyond the torments of the flesh; it is the madwoman who seems to be enduring the punishment. The confusion in intent is further heightened by a return to some very self-conscious prose—an understandable reflex: when writers are not clear about what they are trying to do, they tend to inflate their style.

"Infancy" and "Childhood" (which have also been produced for educational television) are much more successful, although both sound like variations on "The Long Christmas Dinner" and *Our Town*. The time is the turn of the century for both one-acters; the first is set in Central Park in New York City, the other in a small community.

"Infancy" opens with a policeman, like the Stage Manager in *Our Town*, announcing various facts to the audience. Then two baby carriages are wheeled through the park; in them sit two grown-up actors wearing baby clothes. Each "baby" has problems, for the grown-ups do not understand them, nor can the babies communicate to the adult world. Most of what the supposedly experienced and more sensible generation has to say in the course of the comedy is pretty foolish. The babies, for the most part, speak in monosyllables and, here and there, indicate their anger and impatience with their elders, who never tell them what they want or need to know. The grown-ups are eager to cram the babies with information, most of it worthless (in a narrow sense): they try to make their offspring learn the multiplication table and the names of the boroughs, like Dickens' Mr. Gradgrind informing his little pupils that they need to know "Facts, facts, facts." The mystery of the universe, the wonder of life—themes the babies apprehend intuitively—are glossed over for a steady diet of information. At last the tormented babies scream with rage and fall into temper tantrums: the frustration of intelligent creatures unable to express themselves in a way their elders might comprehend. (In the background, the policeman hovers over a governess, dreaming of love.) After the hysterics are over, one baby, showing how much he has learned, shouts in an infant's voice: "I want to have a baby!" And with those words, Wilder suggests that the cycle will begin again.

Lack of communication between generations, not in a physical way, as Wilder demonstrated in "Infancy," but in a psychic one, is the thread that runs through "Childhood." Three children, two sisters and their brother, lose themselves in childhood dreams. Even though their parents are young, to the children they seem remote, ancient. They spend one afternoon playing a game in which they are free to wander where they like, for their parents are dead. At first amused by what the children are doing, the mother and father then show bewilderment and hurt, for they are unable to follow or really enter the game. The children talk about their parents' funeral, their father's worry about money, their mother's nagging. Suddenly they decide to take a trip across the country on a bus, and they supply themselves with new names: they become Mr. Wentworth, Mrs. Arizona, Miss Wilson. Their parents, trying to reach the children by taking part in the game, pretend to be strangers also making the journey: the father becomes the bus driver, the mother a passenger they meet. As the landscape changes according to the father's description (he sounds like Mr. Kirby of "The Happy Journey from Trenton to Camden"), he compares the difficulties of the trip with the ups-and-downs of life. The children, very formal and aloof at first, become more enthusiastic as their parents enter into the game; by the end of the trip both children and grown-ups understand each other a little better. The parents recall their own childhood and its fancies and longings, and have lived it over again for a few moments with the children, while the latter perceive that their parents are really "human, after all."

"Childhood" was received more warmly than the other plays, although some critics were offended by its sentimentality. As a "memory play" it has its own charm, but a more serious criticism of it is its repetition of a theme Wilder had used before and used more effectively. To some extent almost every writer is drawn to a few similar themes over and over again: what is essential is to suggest variations on them. But "Childhood" is a diluted version of *Our Town*. We have been there before, and there are no new revelations.

Temporarily abandoning the cycle of plays for another idea, Wilder retired into isolation and, in 1967, finished and published his novel *The Eighth Day*. It is his longest and most ambitious work of fiction.

In 1952 Friedrich Heer, under the name of Hermann Gode, published a novel called *Der Achte Tag* ("The Eighth Day"). Set in the year 2050, it depicted the lives of Austrian nobility ruined by barbarian hordes. Yet, after the fires had died down and peace finally came, the family could still be found amid the ruins, drinking wine, playing cards, and talking. Unlike George Orwell, who in *1984* predicted the end of humanism, Heer believed that nothing could kill it. Wilder's novel of the same name stands for fundamentally the same things.

Structurally, the book is divided into six chapters and a Prologue. The technique in time resembles that of *The Ides of March:* Chapter One covers the years from 1885 to 1905; Chapter Two moves from 1902 to 1905; Chapter Three covers the same time span as the preceding section; Chapter Four focuses on one year, 1883; Chapter Five returns to the past and encompasses the years from 1880 to 1905; Chapter Six settles on the year with which almost all the other chapters ended, 1905. But this last chapter depicts Christmas of that year.

The chapters also have shifting locales. Thus the first chapter is set in a small town in Illinois; the second moves to Chile, South America; the third to a large city, Chicago; the fourth to the East Coast and Hoboken, New Jersey; the fifth deals with another home in the small Illinois town; and the last involves the whole town (Coaltown) itself, tying together the families studied in Chapters One and Five. In this way more than half of America is covered geographically, and by setting one chapter in South America Wilder takes in the Western Hemisphere. Since one set of characters has close ties to Germany, Europe—or at least its cultural traditions— also forms a part of the novel.

On a third level, each chapter studies the life of a

particular character. The first introduces the reader to John Ashley and his family; the second follows him on his flight to Chile; the third covers the same time span in which his children move to Chicago; the fourth tells us how Ashley came to marry the girl he chose and also provides her history; the fifth gives us the history of a second family, the Lansings, whose fortunes are woven together with those of the Ashleys by both fate and choice; and the last chapter returns to the children of the third section, who have grown older and made a success of their lives. Although this shuttling device superficially suggests *The Ides,* as mentioned, its scope is larger and reminds the reader more of Wilder's plan for his cycle of fourteen plays. Since he had been previously preoccupied with them, its effect on his thinking became discernible in this novel. All the deadly sins and all the ages of man are encompassed in it: *The Eighth Day* may well be Wilder's solution through narrative of what had been a set of dramatic problems.

If *Heaven's My Destination* may be described as an American version of John Bunyan's *Pilgrim's Progress* (the young man in search of his soul), in which George Brush's goal is ironically stated, *The Eighth Day* involves a kind of group voyage (the later novel also begins on a train), during which Dr. Gillies, as a kind of Stage Manager, jokingly explains the title: the eighth day, the day after God rested, when the process of creation and progress resumed. Whether there is really any "progress" is as much a question as George's ultimate destination as he rides toward "heaven." Abandoning the objectivity that had characterized *The Ides,*

Wilder resumes the mantle of author-narrator: he is not a person in the novel but a kind of omniscient being commenting on the scene and posing philosophical questions. Because it is also a "family" novel in its study of several generations—a form of fiction that had gone out of fashion several decades before (the popularity of the television series based on John Galsworthy's *The Forsyte Saga* notwithstanding)—Wilder had to invest the genre with some kind of novelty, and he chose to begin it as a mystery novel:

> In the early summer of 1902 John Barrington Ashley of Coaltown, a small mining center in southern Illinois, was tried for the murder of Breckenridge Lansing, also of Coaltown. He was found guilty and sentenced to death. Five days later, at one in the morning of Tuesday, July 22, he escaped from his guards on the train that was carrying him to his execution.

In the next paragraph we are informed that the trial had been badly bungled, that the convicted murderer vanished into thin air without anyone's help, and that five years later new evidence was uncovered which made it clear that Ashley was innocent. "There had been a miscarriage of justice in an unimportant case in a small Midwestern town."

The most baffling aspects of the case were the failure to establish a motive for the murder and the ineptness of the defense. But what made the case unique was Ashley's escape. It was finally established that he did not lift a finger from beginning to end. He was rescued by six unknown men who entered the car and carried him off. Everything about the event was peculiar: "the strength, the skill, the precision, but above all the silence and the fact that the rescuers were unarmed. It was eerie; it was unearthly."

Naturally the reader's interest is piqued: the novel as it opens has all the earmarks of a "whodunnit." But Wilder is not interested in the solution (which arrives long after the reader has ceased to wonder about it). He uses the rescue from the train exactly as he had used the collapse of the bridge of San Luis Rey. Brother Juniper investigates the reason why a particular group of people perished on a particular day at a particular moment; the narrator of *The Eighth Day* investigates the reason why an insignificant man was freed by six strangers and what the results of that freedom brought.

Although Wilder returned to historical America for his material, he used very little of the political and economic events of the years between 1880 and 1905. There are some contemporary references to certain problems, such as the poor in the workhouses of a big city, the inefficiency and possibly the corruption of the judicial system, the tuberculosis epidemic that broke out at one point. But such subjects as would have delighted the heart of Theodore Dreiser—the financial crisis that occurred in 1893, for example—are not mentioned. Dreiser weighs down his novels with perhaps excessive detail in order to give the reader a photograph of flawless accuracy; Wilder uses details, too, but only in order to prove they are the ingredients that link people together. Details are a form of ritual as he sees it.

Since the focus of the story is to be John Ashley (he is not the leading character, simply the catalyst), it is important to know what manner of man he is. We learn that as a young man he had lost his religious faith and had decided that submission to the will of God involved "some last numbing demand on human fortitude," which he was not prepared to obey. Wilder is careful to point out that Ashley's atheism has tied him to an even greater rigidity of thought and superstition. As the events of the novel sort themselves out, we see that by the end of the story Ashley, another pilgrim on the road of life, regains his faith and with it an understanding of the human mystery. The similarity of the theme to *The Alcestiad* is unmistakable. But Wilder also makes it clear that regaining one's faith is not a matter of rejoining a church—which can be another form of superstition. Nor does faith seem important to the powerful and worldly. But without faith it is impossible to live an active (in the sense of constructive) life, or genuinely to contribute anything to it. The significance of these men of faith is often not apparent to others: their lives are not showy or striking. As Wilder sees it, no "historic demands were laid upon him [John Ashley]; he is to be regarded only as a stitch in a tapestry, a planter of trees, a breaker of stones on an old road to a not yet clearly marked destination." And—another favorite idea of Wilder's, linking genius in art with genius in life—men like John Ashley are a part of "relationships, recurrences, patterns, and laws."

As the story unfolds in the Prologue—the murder of Breckenridge Lansing, the trial of John Ashley, his escape, his sojourn in South America, the breakup of the family, the success of his son Roger as a journalist and his daughter Lily as an opera singer—Wilder raises questions about "Heredity and Environment, about gifts and talents, and destiny and chance." What was there so special about Ashley that

> brought down upon him so mixed a portion of fate: unmerited punishment, a "miraculous" rescue, ex- ile, and an illustrious progeny? What was there in the ancestry and later in the home life of the Ashleys that fostered this energy of mind and spirit? . . . Was there a connection between the catastrophe that befell both houses and these later develop- ments? Are humiliation, injustice, suffering, destitu- tion, and ostracism—are they blessings?

Knowing Wilder, we can be sure that the answer is "Yes."

The Prologue continues with a history of Coaltown beginning with the Indian settlement and ends on December 31, 1899, the last day of the century. Looking forward to the "new age" as ours looks forward to the era ushered in by the landing on the moon, Dr. Gillies and his friends consider the past as the future. Dr. Gillies comments ironically that Man is entering a new stage of development, but the narrator informs us that he is lying: "He had no doubt that the coming century would be too direful to contemplate—that is to say, like all other centuries." Clearly Wilder, while fully aware of the pressures of our time, still believes that *Plus ça change, plus c'est la même chose.* Or, as the conclusion of the church prayer has it, "As it was before, is now and ever will be, world without end, Amen." The background is then set in the succeeding chapters for the investigation: who are the Ashleys and the Lansings; what are they; what have they accomplished; what does all the information add up to; what pattern emerges?

In the first chapter we meet John Ashley and his family. John loved the wife of his friend and partner, Breckenridge Lansing, but never allowed his feelings to interfere with his sense of duty. When the catastrophe falls on the Ashley family and they are left without support, Sophia, his daughter, decides to rent out some of the rooms in their home, "The Elms," and take boarders. Her sister Constance helps. One of the boarders, Ladislas Malcolm, falls in love with the third sister, Lily. Although he is married Lily feels she cannot live without him, and when he leaves to go to Chicago she follows him, hoping at the same time to make a career for herself as a singer. Her brother Roger also sets out for Chicago to seek his fortune, and the family ties are broken.

In the second chapter we follow their father, John Ashley, in his flight to Chile. Once the attempt has been made to rescue him he loses his passivity (which marked his behavior all through the murder trial) and follows the road to freedom. He is described in detail as a man of faith from Wilder's point of view; such people are "fearless, not self-referent, uninteresting, humorless, so often unlearned." It is their very ordinariness that makes them extraordinary. By his act, John has formed a pattern for himself: he refused to surrender, though he had to flee. Adds the author: "We do not choose the day of our birth nor may we choose the day of our death, yet choice is the sovereign faculty of the mind." And he notes that "the spectacle that most discourages people of faith is not error or ignorance or cruelty, but sloth"—that is, a refusal to act, to choose, Wilder's view again of this particular deadly sin.

This section chronicles John's escape, his journey to New Orleans (he has changed his appearance to disguise himself, for his picture has been freely circulated as a criminal wanted for murder; yet, oddly enough, he now "resembles one of the Apostles"); and after various adventures and encounters, he sails for Chile. Maria Icaza, a fortune-teller (she appears in a similar garb in *The Skin of Our Teeth),* informs him, "When God loves a creature He wants the creature to know the highest happiness and the deepest misery—then he can die. He wants him to know all that being alive can bring. That is his best gift . . . . There is no happiness for those who have not looked at the horror and the *nada."*

When John is the witness to various types of suffering, a doctor tells him, "Suffering is like money. It circulates from hand to hand. We pass on what we take in." The comment is an illustrative one, suggesting that Wilder believes the world we live in *is* the world we make. So the evil that raged through Europe before World War II was a reflection of the moral convictions of the people. Put more familiarly, "By their fruits ye shall know them." Again the narrator interrupts the story with a reflection:

the world was a place of cruelty, suffering and confusion, but men and women could surmount despair by making beautiful things, by emulating the beauty of the first creation . . . . We do not know why we suffer, we do not know why millions and millions of people suffer . . . . But only those who have suffered ever come to have a heart that is wise.

At a funeral service for a child John recites the Gettysburg address, *The Village Blacksmith* (Longfellow's poem), and Portia's speech on mercy and justice from *The Merchant of Venice.* And the narrator again reflects, "We cannot understand now what has happened to us . . . . Let us live as though we believed there were some meaning in it." He strikes up an acquaintance with a doctor named McKenzie, who offers an interesting philosophy (possibly Wilder's): "Mothers are no help. Wives are no help. Mistresses are no help. They want to possess the man. They want him to serve their interests. Pallas Athene wants a man to surpass himself." The Goddess of Wisdom, who sprang full-grown from the brain of the father of the gods, is the only patron saint a man can worship.

John becomes interested in the Chilean people and helps to build a church for them, even though he is not, like them, a Catholic. He works to improve the conditions of the miners; he helps them secure the services of a resident priest. His whole time in Chile becomes a kind of reparation for the forced abandonment of his children when he fled from America. Finally, even in Chile he is recognized, but an old woman who has become acquainted with him, and who loves him as if he were her grandchild, helps him to escape. Her faith and her character change John's view of life, enrich his experiences, and force him to find himself. He takes passage for another country and is drowned at sea. But his death does not matter; what matters is *how* he has lived.

Chapter Three covers the same amount of time and is to be taken simultaneously as an account of what happens to John's children in Chicago while he is in Chile. Roger works at various jobs: a night clerk in a hotel, a bank messenger, a hospital orderly, where he watches people die. He has no wish to acquire a formal education, he is suspicious of books. He asks, "What does a college education do?" He is given a characteristic Wilder answer: "It ties together the things that we see." (Notice that for Wilder education is not to be taken as an opportunity to earn a better salary; it is not a "practical" asset but, in the end, a moral and a spiritual one.) Roger's complaint against education is one that is heard increasingly in the world today; he notes that "many of those books and colleges have been around for hundreds of years—with very little effect." (A young student might ask today, "What's *relevant* about books?") But Roger grows tired of experiencing life; he wants to understand it. And so he is drawn toward books as a kind of digestive tablet that will help him assimilate what he has taken in.

He meets an archbishop who tells him about some German missionaries in China. Captured by unfriendly Chinese and placed in separate cells, they nevertheless sent out messages. Men of other nationalities were also imprisoned: Portuguese, English, French. Slowly, gradually, they began tapping out communications to each other in all the languages they knew, even if they could not understand each other. "We are all like the Portuguese: we transmit (we hope) fairer things than we can fully grasp."

Not all of Roger's encounters are spiritual and ethical, philosophical and intellectual. He encounters women (perhaps the least satisfactory part of this chapter from the view of credibility or conviction): the girls are much more symbols than people, for one is a Negress, another an Oriental, etc. And he meets his sister Lily at the opera; through her, he makes the acquaintance of her teacher. He is another mouthpiece through which the author speaks:

> History is the record of man's repeated failures to extricate himself from his incorrigible nature. Those who see progress in it are as deluded as those who see a gradual degeneration. A few steps forward, a few steps back. Human nature is like the ocean, unchanging, changeable. Today's calm, tomorrow's tempest—but it's the same ocean. Man is as he is, as he was, as he always will be . . . . "

And he concludes: "Works of art are the only satisfactory products of civilization."

Lily, who has had an illegitimate child by the man she fell in love with and followed to Chicago, sounds like a member of the "now" generation; she is convinced that marriage is a worn-out custom like owning slaves or adoring royal families. "I believe that there won't be any marriages in a hundred years." And she tells her brother of their missing father who loved people and had friends outside his home but could never mention them to his wife, Beata. Saddest of all, Beata had no room for anyone in her heart except her husband. But she could not communicate with him even though she loved him. At the end of the chapter Roger returns home for Christmas and accidentally meets Felicité Lansing, the daughter of the murdered man. Leaping ahead in time, Roger knows he will marry her, and so bring together the two families that had been split by tragedy.

The next chapter is devoted to Beata, the woman who loved so silently, the mother of these unusual children. Beata's mother, an aristocrat of German ancestry and a snob and bully, had shaped enough of Beata's character to make the girl look on marriage as an escape from parental tyranny. She had eloped with the young John Ashley, who selected her very carefully after eliminating unlikely prospects. But they never married, although they lived as man and wife and raised a family. As for the ceremony, "they never found the time for it"; what bound them was not a piece of paper but the kind of life they had created together. Even if their relationship was an imperfect one, it had reality—the kind Alcestis comes to appreciate in her marriage to Admetus.

The following chapter studies the Lansing family. Lansing's wife, Eustacia, a Creole of good family, had always imagined that she would mate with a demigod. But fate chose otherwise. She fell in love with, and married, Breckenridge Lansing—handsome, charming, empty, a fraud. The character of the Prologue, Dr. Gillies, muses on this contradiction, insisting: "We don't live our lives. Life lives us." The two women—one the wife (at least morally) of John Ashley, the other the ideal of his heart—form an interesting contrast: Beata, with her German parentage, is described as a "child of the ear" with a magic voice (which Lily undoubtedly inherited). Eustacia is Latin (her ancestry being French); she is "a child of the eye" and the mistress of color and design. The son of one marries the daughter of the other, consolidating the best in both. Eustacia, sometimes regretting her life, reflects: "Everything is mysterious, but how unendurable life would be without the mystery." She is not happy with her husband, who has disappointed her. He, in turn, has been shaped into what he is by a father who did not understand him. But when Breck falls ill and Eustacia looks after him, she understands him in a way she never could before. And she realizes that "We come into the world to learn"—an article of faith with Wilder. Just before his death, Breck has his moment of illumination, as did John Ashley before he was drowned at sea.

The last chapter takes place at Christmas, the ritual season for bringing together a scattered family. As Roger Ashley takes the train home from Chicago to visit his mother, the narrator uses the train itself as a means of shifting back and forth in time. He mentions the distant past and Babylon, and from it moves to a date well beyond the span of the book itself, 1930. In that future time we learn that Roger's sister Constance has married a Japanese diplomat and crusaded for women's

rights; that Lily has become a famous opera singer with
a few more illegitimate children; that Roger himself has
blossomed into a well-known writer. The sister who ran
the boardinghouse, Sophia, becomes a nurse—with her
a vocation rather than a profession. It is she who
outlives them all, even into senility: the last stage of
Wilder's Ages of Man cycle. And all these things occurred just because there was once a miscarriage of
justice, because their father was wrongly imprisoned for
murder and escaped to flee his native land.

Only at this point is the truth told about the murder.
Breckenridge Lansing's son George, who was afraid
that his father would harm his mother in one of his
violent, mad rages, is the murderer: he had killed his
father in defense of his mother and run away from
home in terror. Later he fell ill and spent some time in a
sanatorium; hence the delay in learning the truth. He in
turn is smuggled out of the country by a seamstress who
had been a Russian countess before her family lost its
wealth. She succeeds in getting him to her friends in
Russia, where he eventually becomes an actor. But after
1917 no more is heard of him.

And now the mysterious rescue of Roger's father is
explained. Once John Ashley had helped some men
from the Covenant Church with their building (as he
was later to do in Chile). He left a letter with them for
Roger, and in it he tells his son that these men had
helped him to escape. The Deacon who brings the letter
shows Roger a rug and asks him to turn it over. When
Roger does so, he sees that on the underside it is naturally
a mass of knots and of frayed and dangling threads.

This view of the rug, explains the Deacon, is like that of human life. You cannot see the design, for you see it from the "wrong" side.

The symbolic significance of the Covenant People is that they claim to be descended from Abraham Lincoln, who freed the slaves. The Elder (and narrator) affirms that it is a mistake of the Jews and Christians to suppose there is only one Messiah. "Every man and woman is Messiah-bearing, but some are closer on the tree to a Messiah than others."

The book concludes with a few other reflections. Hell is seen as the place where there is no hope or possibility of change. And the last, relevant question is raised: "Is America, who so wronged the Indian, singled out for so high a destiny?" The novel's theme is tied together by a statement shortly before the conclusion: "History is *one* tapestry. No eye can venture to compass more than a hand's-breadth . . . . "

Wilder has obviously thought deeply about the problems that rack the world today. What is the use of books that teach us about right conduct if we never apply the lessons? Are the concepts of family life we have so long held really doomed to extinction? Will our world as we know it go the way of Babylon and become another lost civilization because of the worship of materialism? Will we be worthy of our dream, "America was Promises," or will we continue to betray those whom we have oppressed and mistreated? Wilder raises the questions, but only we, the human race, individually, can supply the answers.

Practically every theme he has ever treated, every idea he has ever had, every technique he has ever used, is worked into *The Eighth Day.* It is a complete summation of his life as a man of letters. It is *his* tapestry. It affirms the same concept found in Richard Wagner's *Ring* cycle, which begins at the bottom of the Rhine and follows the fortunes of the people who struggle for power and the destruction of Valhalla, home of the gods, by fire. At the end, the final music from *Götterdämmerung,* the last opera in the cycle, is heard: it is a repetition of the opening music of the first opera, *Das Rheingold.* The tempest is over, the water ripples under the breeze, and the universe is ready for another beginning.

Despite the scope of the novel and the greatness of its theme—nothing more or less than Life itself—it is one of Wilder's less successful efforts. The felicity of style, so apparent in *The Ides of March,* is missing. The complaint, as far back as *The Bridge of San Luis Rey,* that the author was intent on piling up proof that some kind of design existed in the universe seems much more warranted here. Everything that occurs in *The Eighth Day* seems to be another piece of evidence about the meaning of life. No loose ends are permitted; the neatness is almost suffocating. For example, both Ashley and Lansing are given their moment of illumination about themselves; after they reach it, they die. (So did the people in *The Bridge,* of course, but at least physically it was possible for all of them to be killed simultaneously because of their presence on the bridge.) It becomes too coincidental for the two men in *The Eighth Day* to perish so far from each other, under such totally different conditions, in such totally different ways—and for no particular *human* reason. This time they seem to have been eliminated by the author because *he* had no further use for them: their death became a kind of punctuation mark in the story he was weaving. Slowly the reader grows aware of Wilder treating his characters like puppets, manipulating them for his own ends—and rather clumsily for a writer of his grace and skill.

Curiously enough, the tidiness of his planning is in sharp contrast to his statement that we cannot understand life completely, since the book hints not only that we can but that we do—or at least the major characters do. As a result the entire novel seems fabricated: its joints and articulations show. Wilder creates the effect of having the answer before he has even asked the question, possibly a useful pedagogical device in the classroom but not a very satisfactory one artistically. The aphorisms dominate the book to such an extent that the lives of the characters become mere interludes whose only purpose is to connect the didactic passages. This, his most consciously "moral" work, is more a treatise on philosophy than a novel.

It is interesting to note that in this period of literary activity Wilder returned to the themes which had most attracted him at the beginning of his career. Tradition in the form of the classics appears with *The Ides of March;* tradition in the form of Americana appears with *The Eighth Day.* If he is more concerned with the cosmic than he was when he was occupied with *Heaven's My Destination* or *The Long Christmas Dinner,* he makes emphatic use of the details that bring his subject matter down to earth. The canvas has broadened, but the colors are still the same.

6 THE DESIGN:
We Come into the World to Learn

Glenway Wescott's sketch of Thornton Wilder the man is a clue to Thornton Wilder the writer. Wescott notes:

> The three of his physical characteristics that especially please me and amuse me are of today and of the past alike.—A singular way of laughing, forcible but not loud, expressing as a rule (I think) a general joy of living rather than a sense of fun at the time and in the circumstances. A flashing of his eyes once in a while; the occasion perhaps suddenly seeming to him a great occasion, or an emergency in some way. Certain emphatic manual, digital gestures when he talks, somewhat in the manner of clergymen of a past generation or of old-time political campaigners.

And elsewhere Wescott sums up his impression:

> At times he made me think of a boy climbing a tree, carefully placing his feet on limb above limb, finally

peering into a bird's nest containing eggs or little birds, and holding his breath, in order not to sully anything with his human odor, not to disillusion or disincline the parent birds when they got back.

And Tyrone Guthrie adds his own observations:

I never met anyone with so encyclopedic a knowledge of so wide a range of topics. Yet he carries this learning lightly, and imparts it—the important with the trivial, the commonplace with the exceedingly bizarre . . . in a style and with a gusto which is all his own . . . . He has been everywhere and has known—and knows—everyone . . . .

And Garson Kanin mentions Wilder's tastes: he likes resorts out of season, such at St. Moritz in early November or Florida in the summer. When he is at home in Hamden he goes to the corner drugstore for breakfast or sits at the lunch counter. And he uses loose-leaf notebooks when he writes his novels and plays. When he hears a story that might be made the theme of a book, he is hesitant about using it too obviously: he shrinks from the risk of hurting or irresponsibly influencing people, from invading their privacy. As his character Sabina says in *The Skin of Our Teeth:* "I don't think the theatre is a place where people's feelings ought to be hurt."

The full-length portrait that emerges from the comments of Wilder's friends is as instantly recognizable as his style. Essentially Wilder is a happy man, and his books are all affirmative in their tone (the bright rather than the dark). The revivalist preacher manner he suggests in company is carried over into his writing: sometimes the results are too emphasized, as in *The Eighth Day;* sometimes they are subtly presented, as in *The Ides of March.* But the message is always there.

The boy examining the bird's nest with breathless awe is probably Wilder's most characteristic stance. Like the very young, he has never lost his sense of wonder, of discovery; and like the very young, he is not bored by the commonplace. When a child asks where the rain comes from or where the sunlight goes, he is asking questions about subjects which are so routine to an adult (yet so basic to life) that an answer hardly seems worthwhile. But the miracle of existence which surrounds the young, and which they forget as they move further from the east—to use Wordsworth's term— never ceases to occupy the center of Wilder's speculations; consequently, although all his themes are rooted in the ordinary, they carry with them a perception that ranges beyond the five senses.

Guthrie's summation of Wilder's incredible fund of knowledge is also characteristic of his style. Even in a lesser novel, such as *The Eighth Day,* the range of his learning remains impressive, not because there is any particular merit in "bookishness" but because Wilder uses his erudition as a device to connect past ages with the present and to show the indebtedness of one era to another. In truth, where would the knowledge of the ancient world be without the patient efforts of the humble, anonymous copyists of the Dark Ages who preserved tradition until the world was again in a fit state to receive it? And for Wilder books are important in another way: they are *explications de texte*—footnotes necessary to interpret life.

Even his preference for famous resorts "out of season" is an indication of the individuality of his point of view. As in his life, so in his literary style and subject matter he has tended to follow his own interests and remain apart from artistic movements that may be popular at the time. Thus, when most American writers were busy offering portraits of real people or slice-of-life situations, Wilder was concentrating on the long ago and the far away, not, indeed, to escape reality but rather to heighten it; as he himself has said, "A writer's job is to describe human beings—no more, no less."

Perhaps he is best understood when we examine his concept of the novelist's function. Wilder sees a writer as a *Menschenkenner*—that is, an artist who understands intuitively the workings of the mind and feels the mystery of life and of human emotion. Consequently, Wilder sees the novelist as all-knowing, holding *all* the strands of a story in his hands (like God), above and outside of his characters and their situations. Put another way, the novelist is not walking along the street as he tells his story: he is flying above the clouds, able to perceive the entire topography and therefore best able to describe the total condition. Naturally enough, Wilder is unreceptive to the kind of clinical psychology that characterizes a good deal of modern fiction, nor does he believe that man can be so simply explained in terms of cause and effect as some scientists would have us suppose.

If the writer, like God, can soar above the average

vision, there has to be some use to which this ability can be put. And here Wilder emerges as a serious moralist. In most of his books and plays he tends to stress the role of teacher or of student. George Brush belongs to the second group, Julius Caesar to the first. But Chrysis in her own way teaches Pamphilus the mystery of life when she defines the bright and the dark; and he, in turn, serves his apprenticeship as her student. The old and worldly Marquesa learns from the simple Pepita; Samuele learns from his experience with the Cabalists; Emily, on her return from death, learns a little of the meaning of life. This particular process is Wilder's most passionate concern.

If learning is man's most important function, Wilder is realistic enough to recognize that, sadly, sometimes the knowledge comes too late. This is why most of his characters, having had their moment of understanding, having learned the lessons they were sent into the world for, cease to exist. Almost without exception, in Wilder's books illumination is instantly followed by death. Far from being a cheerful optimist, Wilder shows himself as one conscious of the terrible waste that marks human activity.

Yet the very fact that man can learn, can profit from his experience, even at the moment of his death, becomes proof that there is some order in the universe, some pattern, some design. Nothing is haphazard. And if there is a design, there must be a Creator of it, called God, Mind, Nature—the name is unimportant. This Being is not to be understood as restricted to any one nation or race or religion, for Wilder has very little patience with *empty* ritual. By weaving time and religion together, in fact, Wilder shows how universal and similar all faiths are: there is more in belief that unites men than separates them.

Possibly this hunger to communicate his belief in an eternal order sometimes weakens Wilder's style. His tendency to use characters as demonstrations of his arguments frequently robs them of memorable qualities. Although Wilder insists that he is not interested in particularizing people, that he wants them to represent eternal symbols, the fact remains that his two best novels, *Heaven's My Destination* and *The Ides of March,* deal with two men who are drawn very particularly indeed. And, in stressing the notion of a divine plan somewhere, he also tends to concentrate so excessively on detail (as in *The Eighth Day*) that he wearies the reader, for his arguments are always in favor of his case and never against it.

It is natural, then, that the "bright" side should be presented most attractively and most skillfully; the "dark" side, though it is much mentioned, hardly ever carries conviction (the major exception is *The Ides of March*). We know the dark is there because Wilder has told us so, but he removes all the drama and the anguish from the picture and simply recounts them from a distance. Pain, for him, is largely theoretical, a dark thread in the tapestry, real but negligible. He is not smug about pain; he simply accepts it.

Yet his virtues as a writer are considerable. The simplicity of his style, when he is at his best, the integrity of his vision, the dedication to his craft, the high purpose of his calling, the individuality of his nature are, in their way, unique. If he does not scale the heights (perhaps lacking the passion, to use Nathaniel Hawthorne's definition, to say "No, in thunder!", certainly unable to share William Faulkner's belief that "to write well about some place, you've got to hate it"), Wilder at least shows us green valleys that we either forget about or take for granted too often. He sums up his own feelings very simply:

> The art of literature springs from two curiosities, a curiosity about human beings pushed to such an extreme that it resembles love, and a love of a few masterpieces of literature so absorbing that it has all the richest elements of curiosity. I use the word *curiosity* in the French sense of a tireless awareness of things . . . . We live in an age where pity and charity have taken on the colors of condescensions; where humility is foolishness and curiosity is interference. Today, hope and faith itself implies deliberate self-deception.

The message that he brings is an old one; his special talent lies in trying to find different and new forms for what he has to say. In his love for tradition and meaning he looks to the past; in his curiosity about the universe he looks to the future. If it is at all possible to put old wine into new bottles, then Thornton Wilder has achieved his purpose.

A SELECTED BIBLIOGRAPHY*

Plays, Novels, and Articles by Wilder

PLAYS

THE TRUMPET SHALL SOUND. *Yale Literary Magazine* (October 1919–January 1920. 4 Volumes.)

THE ANGEL THAT TROUBLED THE WATERS. New York: Coward-McCann, Inc., 1928.

THE LONG CHRISTMAS DINNER AND OTHER PLAYS. New York: Coward-McCann, Inc., 1931.

LUCRÈCE. Translated from the French of André Obey. Boston: Houghton, Mifflin, 1933.

OUR TOWN. New York: Harper & Brothers, 1938.

THE MERCHANT OF YONKERS. New York: Harper & Brothers, 1939.

*Unless otherwise noted, all entries are first editions.

THE SKIN OF OUR TEETH. New York: Harper & Brothers, 1942.

THE MATCHMAKER. New York: Harper & Brothers, 1955.

THE ALCESTIAD; THE DRUNKEN SISTERS. Published only in German as *"Die Alkestiade," Schauspiel in drei Akten mit einem Satyrspiel, "Die Beschwipsten Schwestern."* Translated by H. E. Herlitschka. Frankfurt: Fischer Bucherei, 1960.

CHILDHOOD. *The Atlantic Monthly,* CCVI (November 1960), pp. 78–84.

NOVELS

THE CABALA. New York: Albert & Charles Boni, 1926.

THE BRIDGE OF SAN LUIS REY. New York: Albert & Charles Boni, 1927.

THE WOMAN OF ANDROS. New York: Albert & Charles Boni, 1930.

HEAVEN'S MY DESTINATION. New York: Harper & Brothers, 1935 (first American edition).

THE IDES OF MARCH. New York: Harper & Brothers, 1948.

THE EIGHTH DAY. New York: Harper & Row, Publishers, 1967.

ARTICLES

"Toward an American Language." *The Atlantic Monthly,* CXC (July 1952), pp. 29–37.

"The American Loneliness." *The Atlantic Monthly,* CXC (August 1952), pp. 65–69.

"Emily Dickinson." *The Atlantic Monthly,* CXC (November 1952), pp. 43–48.

Works About Wilder and His Times

BURBANK, REX. *Thornton Wilder.* New York: Twayne publishers, 1961.

CAMPBELL, JOSEPH, AND ROBINSON, HENRY M. "The Skin of Whose Teeth?", *Saturday Review of Literature,* XXV (December 19, 1942), pp. 3–4.

COWLEY, MALCOLM. Introduction to *A Thornton Wilder Trio.* New York: Criterion Books, 1956.

FERGUSSON, FRANCIS. "Three Allegorists: Brecht, Wilder and Eliot," The *Sewanee Review,* LXIV (Fall 1956), pp. 544–73.

FIREBAUGH, JOSEPH. "The Humanism of Thornton Wilder," *The Pacific Spectator,* IV (Autumn 1950), pp. 426–28.

FULLER, EDMUND. "Reappraisals: Thornton Wilder: 'The Notation of the Heart,'" *The American Scholar,* XXVIII (Spring 1959), pp. 210-17.

GASSNER, JOHN. *Form and Idea in Modern Theatre.* New York: The Dryden Press, 1956.

GOLD, MICHAEL. "Prophet of the Genteel Christ," *The New Republic,* LXIV (October 22, 1930), pp. 266–67.

GOLDSTEIN, MALCOLM. *The Art of Thornton Wilder.* The University of Nebraska Press, 1965.

GUTHRIE, TYRONE. *A Life in the Theatre.* New York: McGraw-Hill Publishing Co., 1959.

HABERMAN, DONALD. *The Plays of Thornton Wilder.* Middletown, Conn.: Wesleyan University Press, 1967.

KANIN, GARSON. *Remembering Mr. Maugham.* New York: Atheneum Publishers, 1966.

KOHLER, DAYTON. "Thornton Wilder," *English Journal,* XXVIII (January 1939), pp. 1–11.

McNamara, Robert. "Phases of American Religion in Thornton Wilder and Willa Cather," *The Catholic World,* CXXXV (September 1932), pp. 641–49.

Nelson, Robert. *Play Within a Play.* New Haven: Yale University Press, 1958.

Papajewski, Helmut. *Thornton Wilder.* New York: Frederick Ungar Publishing Co., 1968.

Sturzl, Erwin. "Weltbild und Lebensphilosophie Thornton Wilders," *Die Neueren Sprachen,* Heft 8, 1955, pp. 341–51.

Wescott, Glenway. *Images of Truth.* New York: Harper & Row, 1962.

Wilder, Amos Niven. *Spiritual Aspects of the New Poetry.* New York: Harper & Brothers, 1940.

Wilson, Edmund. *The Shores of Light.* New York: Farrar, Straus & Young, 1952.

INDEX

ABOUT THE AUTHOR

M. C. Kuner is an associate professor of English at Hunter College in New York, where she teaches courses in literature and drama. A graduate of Hunter College, she received her master's degree from Yale University and her Ph.D. from Columbia University. Her major interests and studies have been in playwriting and theater history, and in 1959 she received a Fullbright Fellowship to do theater research at the University of Vienna.

Miss Kuner is the author of an original play, *Capacity for Wings,* which was produced off-Broadway and at various universities in the United States and England. She has received the Anderson Award for Playwriting given by Stanford University and the Sergel Award for the Best Play of the Year given by the Dramatic Publishing Company and the University of Chicago. As a student at the Yale School of Drama, she met Thornton Wilder and remembers well his kindness and genuine interest in young playwrights whose work was being produced at the school.

Miss Kuner lives in New York City.